THE ENCYCLOPEDIA OF

fashion
illustration techniques

THE ENCYCLOPEDIA OF

fashion

illustration techniques

CAROL A. NUNNELLY

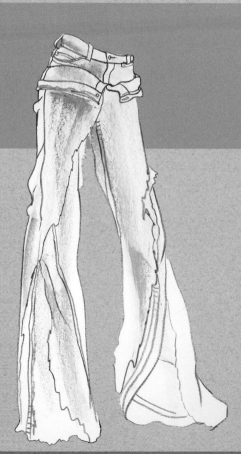

RUNNING PRESS
PHILADELPHIA · LONDON

A QUARTO BOOK

Copyright © 2009 Quarto Inc.

First published in the United States in 2009
by Running Press Book Publishers

9 8 7 6 5 4 3 2 1
Digit on the right indicates the number
of this printing

Library of Congress Control Number:
2008936448

ISBN: 978-0-7624-3576-0

Conceived, designed, and produced by
Quarto Publishing plc
The Old Brewery
6 Blundell Street
London N7 9BH

Senior editor: Liz Dalby
Art director: Caroline Guest
Managing art editor: Anna Plucinska
Designer: Elizabeth Healey
Picture researcher: Sarah Bell
Design assistant: Saffron Stocker
Photographers: Martin Norris, Phil Wilkins
Additional illustrations: Danielle Meder
Additional caption text: Caroline Tatham
Creative director: Moira Clinch
Publisher: Paul Carslake

Running Press Book Publishers
2300 Chestnut Street
Philadelphia, PA 19103-4371

Visit us on the web!
www.runningpress.com

Contents

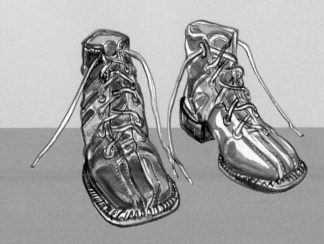

Foreword

Draw, design, sew, and create. This is the philosophy behind good fashion design and illustration instruction. Drawing and illustrating well will give you an edge in today's competitive market. This book teaches you the important steps used to create fashion illustrations in a variety of media. The key to your success is to take stock of your skills and evaluate what you need to learn. If you develop yourself and learn to overcome your weaknesses, you can work effectively in your chosen field. If you are a designer, this book will help you use efficient methods of working to save time and allow you to gain the satisfaction of knowing you can depict a croquis figure in your portfolio with ease. If your goal is to be a better fashion illustrator, this book shows you how to experiment with media and follow a logical methodology of depicting folds, the body, and expression; and become a great draftsman. When you are able to draw beautifully fit clothing on an exquisitely drawn figure, you will find that the powerful expression of your work resonates with your viewers.

This guide will help you with specific points of illustration including drawing hands, feet, and figures from head to toe. You will also gain valuable knowledge in drawing and rendering techniques including color harmony tips. The fashion silhouette and many important points of drawing accessories as well as fashion proportions are discussed. Remember: to draw with authority is to draw with brevity, using a bold and direct line. Editing a drawing and "pushing" your expression while drawing and illustrating well from the beginning idea to the finished illustration, is a process that involves following the guidelines in this book and then picking and choosing what works for you.

Carol A. Nunnelly

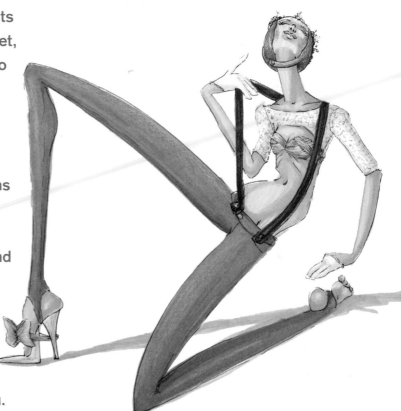

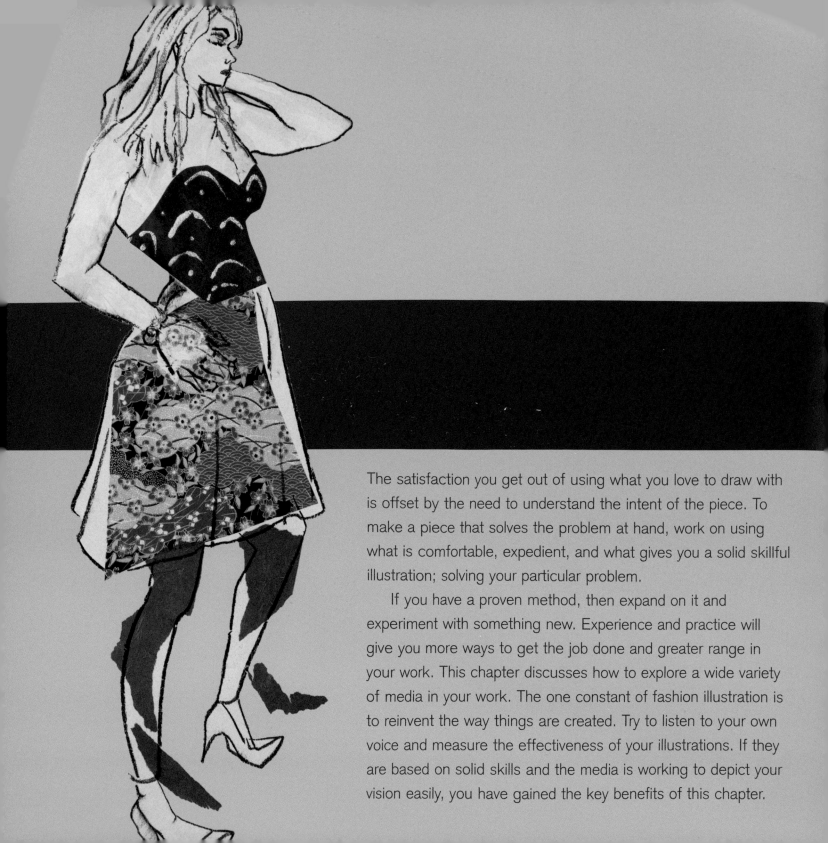

The satisfaction you get out of using what you love to draw with is offset by the need to understand the intent of the piece. To make a piece that solves the problem at hand, work on using what is comfortable, expedient, and what gives you a solid skillful illustration; solving your particular problem.

If you have a proven method, then expand on it and experiment with something new. Experience and practice will give you more ways to get the job done and greater range in your work. This chapter discusses how to explore a wide variety of media in your work. The one constant of fashion illustration is to reinvent the way things are created. Try to listen to your own voice and measure the effectiveness of your illustrations. If they are based on solid skills and the media is working to depict your vision easily, you have gained the key benefits of this chapter.

CHAPTER *1*

Media

DRY MEDIA

Monochrome

Monochrome media includes graphite pencils, charcoal, and charcoal pencils. Charcoal can be rubbed and smudged and is excellent for showing strong light and shadow effects and creating the illusion of form. A graphite pencil is perfect for an initial sketch or for showing contour outlines. This is the tool you will use most often as a fashion designer or illustrator.

CHARCOAL AND CHARCOAL PENCIL

You will likely use charcoal extensively to draw form, folds, and light and shadow effects. Shapes and values are easy to achieve in this black and white medium that offers both line and tonal application techniques.

Techniques: Line-drawing and shape; smudged texture; collage drawing; light and shadow effects.

Buying guide: Charcoal and charcoal pencils are available in hard and soft grades—hard charcoal is lighter in value but will not smear, while soft charcoal is darker and can be smudged easily. Charcoal pencils are difficult to sharpen—use a knife to keep a point.

Paper: Large format paper is easiest to use when drawing with charcoal. Because charcoal is a soft medium, smaller paper will make a smeared charcoal line appear much too big. Charcoal looks good on either white or toned paper.

Strengths: Charcoal is a "workhorse" medium and a great choice for drawing a live model. The lines are fluid, bold, and can be varied in weight to create a strong illusion of form and volume.

Drawbacks: Charcoal smudges easily so it is difficult to keep the paper clean. Charcoal pencil lines will not erase. Wet media are not easy to apply over a charcoal line without smearing the line and creating a messy, gray, smudged appearance.

Ease of use: Easy.

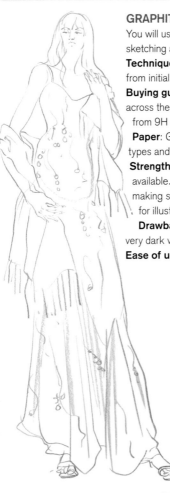

GRAPHITE PENCIL

You will use graphite pencils extensively for sketching and finished pieces.

Techniques: Good for all forms of illustration, from initial sketches to finished outlines.

Buying guide: Collect a range of pencils across the different grades that are available, from 9H (hardest) to 9B (softest).

Paper: Graphite pencil can be used on all types and sizes of papers.

Strengths: Pencils are cheap and readily available. They are easy to carry around for making sketches at the planning stage, or for illustrating and refining later work.

Drawbacks: It is not possible to achieve a very dark value line with a graphite pencil.

Ease of use: Easy.

Pencil details

This example shows how well pencil depicts details. The line weight is varied to add interest, and the drawing has a finished appearance. Color would enhance the drawing but is not essential. When faced with a deadline, a well drawn pencil illustration can stand alone.

Folds and form

This example of charcoal drawing shows how well the media depicts the depths and form of folds and the softness of fabric. Notice how well the charcoal lines give the illusion of thick and thin fabric through a varied line weight.

2 Colored pencils

Colored pencils can be used alone or combined with other media; they are great for details and contour outlines of figure or clothing. Applying a base layer of marker or watercolors followed by colored pencils for details is a popular technique. The waxy surface texture of colored pencil—when applied heavily—is a permanent surface; colored pencil lines do not erase easily.

Graphite and color
This drawing illustrates how well graphite pencils combine with watercolor. The pencil line was the first layer on the white paper. A wash was applied over the top to create more depth and color interest.

Techniques: Contour lines; details; surface texture for fabric rendering; marker drawing; watercolor; sketches.

Buying guide: Colored pencils are available in a wide variety of colors. The best approach is to buy a set and add to this by purchasing additional colors as you need them. It's worth investing in a specially designed pencil case to organize a lot of colors.

Paper: All types of paper work well with colored pencils; use them on any color or weight of paper. Watercolor pencils work better with a thicker paper. Generally, when using pencils you should select a small-format paper because the lines you make are quite thin. You can use larger format paper, but contour lines will appear less bold. Sketchbooks are the perfect place to use colored pencils.

Strengths: Pencil lines are excellent for showing details. Contour lines are sharp, and colored pencils come in a wide variety of colors.

Drawbacks: A few colored pencils are not enough to make a difference to your illustration—you'll need to buy a large set, and the initial outlay may be high. Pencils don't erase and are very waxy if applied too thickly. Although you can use them on large-format paper, colored pencils are best used on smaller format paper or in a sketchbook.

Ease of use: Easy. A layered approach—using colored pencils to add details over a base layer of watercolor or marker—is a technique you will often use.

▭ TURN THE PAGE For more media examples

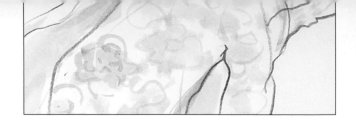

Paint

Watercolors are excellent for blended color, achieved by applying colors over clear water. Or, aim for a looser application with paint drips, splatters, and surprise effects. Gouache is opaque watercolor that can be used alone or combined with other media. It works well when applied over transparent watercolor or marker, and a light-toned gouache will even cover a darker-toned paper.

Unpredictable effects

The random and often unpredictable results created when watercolor drips and runs are part of the appeal of this media. By using wet-in-wet or dry-brush techniques you can get many great texture and color results. Watercolor paint is not permanent and will dissolve with water even after it is dry, so care in handling the finished illustration is necessary. When applying layers, a deft touch is needed to avoid muddy color effects and over-blended areas of paint.

WATERCOLOR

Techniques: Fabric rendering; dripped paint; light and shadow effects; wet-in-wet; dry-brush.

Buying guide: The initial choice is between tubes or pan colors that come in a set. For ease of use, pan colors are more workable. For better quality color and pigment, or for mixing larger quantities of paint, choose tubes.

Paper: White paper is recommended; you will want to take advantage of the luminous quality of the paint by building up transparent layers on the background. Thick watercolor paper is best; the water will cause thinner paper to buckle.

Strengths: Excellent for creating a vibrant and luminous surface appearance and for loose illustration styles.

Drawbacks: Watercolor paint does not dry permanent so, when applying layers, you need to use quick, light strokes. It is difficult to mix up large amounts of colors from pans.

Ease of use: Moderately easy.

Dry brush technique
This figure illustrates dry brush technique on the pants and shows how loose, quick color application can give a drawing immediacy.

Delicate detailing
The dress and hair show the delicate quality of watercolor and how it can be applied with ease to show patterns or body color.

Light-over-dark layering

Gouache paint is a valuable tool in that it allows you to create dark-over-light value effects or light-over-dark rendering, using a layered approach. Colored gouache paint in a light value will easily cover a toned background paper surface of a darker value. Gouache paint does not dry permanently though, and care needs to be taken upon completion of the rendering to avoid ruining the paint surface.

GOUACHE

Techniques: Pattern rendering; details; accessories; toned paper rendering.

Buying guide: Buying a few paints in order to mix a full color range requires a selection of key colors. These include: Permanent White, Ivory Black, Flame Red (warm), Bengal Rose (cool), Turquoise Blue (warm), Ultramarine Blue (cool), Cadmium Yellow Pale (warm), and Lemon Yellow (cool). From these basic colors, you can mix all the colors you will need.

Paper: Gouache paint can work on small or large format paper. A variety of surfaces are also possible, including the following paper types: white drawing paper, watercolor paper, Bristol paper, and toned paper.

Strengths: Gouache paints are opaque and vibrant. They produce a richly colored rendering with an attractive, velvety surface to the dried paint.

Drawbacks: Gouache does not dry permanent and a single drop of water on a finished piece can ruin the painted surface.

Ease of use: Moderate.

You will tend to use gouache paint from time to time in your illustration work.

Gouache on toned paper
This example shows how well opaque gouache covers a toned background paper. With one coat of paint application, the color is complete.

▭▷ **TURN THE PAGE** For more media examples

WET MEDIA

4 Ink

Black ink applied with a brush gives a beautiful line quality. The fluid line and the ease of application are the strengths of this medium. It also works well with other techniques including dry pastel and watercolor or colored ink washes. Colored inks give a vibrant effect and behave in a similar way to watercolor paints. They are also available in metallic finishes.

BLACK INK

Techniques: Details; life drawing; fluid and varied line weights; watercolor; dry pastel.

Buying guide: Black ink is available in permanent and non-permanent versions. If you intend to use layers and draw overlay colors in another wet medium, use permanent ink.

Paper: All papers—including toned papers— work well with black ink. Heavyweight papers are best when using wet media to ensure the surface does not buckle.

Strengths: Black ink is ideal for handling complex and delicate details as well as long and simple fluid lines. Creating variety in line quality is easy with a brush and ink.

Drawbacks: It is not easy to control the fluid nature of marks made using a brush and ink. Ink illustration and drawing is best done quickly and with a deft touch. It can be hard to control the proportion of a drawing.

Ease of use: Easy.

Bold lines
This figure was illustrated using bold ink lines. You can see here how the details of the face— requiring small marks—and the longer lines depicting the legs—requiring more fluid brushstrokes—are handled equally adeptly with this medium.

Added color
A brush and ink drawing form the details of the clothing and the model's pose as a first layer. Additional color was added to this drawing in watercolor for a layer that supplies more information about surface texture and color. Although this drawing is not heavily colored, you can see how more or less watercolor application will not detract from the original layer.

Blended effects

Inks mix together to create interesting results when
one color is dropped into another in the "wet-in-wet"
method. Inks behave in a similar manner to watercolor
paints but differ in the way they create a blended wash. Ink-
blended effects are fantastically abstract, and are especially
effective when used to depict shiny fabrics such as satin or
vinyl. Acrylic ink dries permanent while other colored inks do
not. Acrylic ink is also available in metallic colors that give a
shine and sparkle to your illustrations.

COLORED INK

Techniques: Fabric rendering; wet-in-wet;
textures; accessory illustrations.
Buying guide: Buy a few basic ink colors first. These can be
mixed to give a greater range of colors. Metallic colors—gold,
bronze, and silver—are also available.
Paper: Heavyweight white paper works best with ink.
Because colors lie on top of the paper they benefit from
the white background. Bristol, watercolor, or heavier
drawing paper are the optimum choices.
Strengths: Ink is an excellent medium to use for accessories or for
any shiny surface textures you want to create in fabric rendering.
Drawbacks: It is difficult to control the bleed effects of ink.
Allowing it to blend while you relax the control is the key to success.
If washes look unattractively colored and are overly textured it is
possible to get an overworked look in your illustration.
Ease of use: Moderately difficult.

Color reaction
This illustration shows how two ink
colors placed together have reacted—
the blended result creates a surface
texture and a color that is perfect for
shiny fabric.

Light and shadow
This figure is illustrated with ink and
demonstrates how well light and
shadow are depicted. The form of
the dress is apparent through the
use of darker and lighter ink colors.

 TURN THE PAGE For more media examples

WET MEDIA

Pens

Using colored markers will give you an immediate effect that can be layered and combined with pencils for maximum color and texture. Gel pens can help you create opaque and detailed effects on an illustration that has a rendered and fully colored surface. They usually provide the final accent layers over a mixed media illustration.

Full color range

To use markers well, you need a wide selection for full color and value effects. Markers can be blended with a marker blender, which looks like a clear, colorless marker. They dry out quickly and need to be used soon after purchase.

MARKERS

You will likely use markers frequently in your fashion illustration work.

Techniques: Fabric rendering; body rendering; faces; small-format illustrations.

Buying guide: The initial outlay for a wide selection of colors and a marker case is likely to be high. A set that includes all the colors and some grays will give you the most range in your work. You will need a case or container to keep the markers handy and organized. You can overlap colors to get more range from a set that has a minimal number of markers.

Paper: White paper of any weight works well for marker drawing. It is best to use Bristol paper since this is a wet medium and needs to have a surface that is heavy enough to allow for overlaying of colors.

Strengths: Markers are a quick-to-apply, layered technique. Although classified as a wet medium, they dry rapidly and can be applied with one layer over another in a matter of minutes.

Drawbacks: Markers dry up easily and you have to use them quickly.

Ease of use: Easy.

Full-color illustration
Using markers gives you the opportunity to move quickly and illustrate in full color with ease. This example shows marker illustration on flesh tones where the form of the body shows a light and shadow effect. See how well the pale gray marker works on white fabric rendering in the T-shirt and sweater to maintain a light effect.

Final layer

The layered approach used in many fashion illustrations makes gel pens a good choice for a bright or light color that would otherwise not show up over a darker under-layer. Gel pens come in a wide variety of colors and are best used over watercolor or marker layers.

GEL PENS

You will use gel pens extensively.

Techniques: Accents; details; pattern rendering; face rendering; highlights; sequins and sparkle rendering; combining with markers or watercolors.

Buying guide: White is the main gel pen to buy; metallic colors are also very useful.

Paper: Any format of paper works with gel pens, and you can also use a range of types, from plain white drawing paper, to watercolor paper, Bristol paper, and also toned paper.

Strengths: Gel pens make an excellent choice for showing jewelry and accessories. They are quick to use for an immediate effect.

Drawbacks: Gel pens clog easily and dry out quickly.

Ease of use: Easy.

Sparkling accents
This red dress was rendered by first applying a red ink to the background of the dress fabric. A silver gel pen was used to draw the patterned sparkled trim.

▷ TURN THE PAGE For more media examples

WET/DRY MEDIA

Pastels

Oil pastels are vibrant and waxy and give a bold effect. They can be used alone or in combination with watercolor washes. Soft pastels are dry and may be used alone or combined with brush and ink or charcoal lines. They smudge easily and the finished illustration may need to be sprayed with fixative to protect it.

OIL PASTELS

You will tend to use oil pastels moderately for painterly, form-filled, or bold line illustrations.

Techniques: Line drawing; shapes—blending with turpenoid; resist when combined with watercolor; patterns and collage drawing; sparing out white ground.

Buying guide: Sets available offer a wide selection of colors and are the best value. It is easy to buy individual oil pastels if you need unique colors. For example, buy extra colors for a metallic color scheme.

Paper: Oil pastel is best used on large-format paper to match the boldness of the lines produced. A thicker and heavier paper is best if you are using oil pastels in combination with turpenoid, because the layers applied will tend to need more support. Toned paper or white paper are both ideal for this versatile medium.

Strengths: Drawing from a live model on large-format paper, there is not a better choice of medium than oil pastel. You can easily create powerful and bold lines that communicate well, and the colors are beautiful.

Drawbacks: It is hard to sharpen an oil pastel to a point, and the line created is thicker than with some other media.

If you enjoy controlled and detailed drawing, you may not like using oil pastels for a delicate detail such as a hand. If you use turpenoid to dissolve the pigment this can result in a buildup of color in layers, and a slightly overworked pigment application. The solution is to remain deft in your touch and avoid all overworking when drawing with a painterly or layered technique.

Ease of use: Line drawing with oil pastel is moderately easy. Painterly effects, using turpenoid with oil pastel, are more difficult.

Graphic lines

The lines in this illustration are bold and graphic. Oil pastel is an ideal medium when drawing in lines; it gives you the ability to draw with color in a quick sketch because without having to fill the shapes, you still have a complete picture.

Painterly effect

Oil pastels are excellent when you wish to create a painterly effect, with pigment application that is rich and textured. This effect can be achieved through layering and by overlapping the colors. The technique of sparing out white can be observed in this example—some of the white paper is not covered by pigment, which adds freshness.

Smudged effects

Using soft pastels enables you to get a full color and value effect and create a feeling for form by using light and shadow. The smudged quality of the medium means you will need to take care to preserve the neatness of the background paper and keep the drawing clean. Spray fixative is often used to preserve the drawing upon completion.

SOFT PASTELS

You will tend to use dry pastels moderately for specific techniques.

Techniques: Fold drawing; smudged texture; light and shadow effects; sparing out the background color.

Buying guide: Select a set that contains at least two values of each color—a light and dark—to enable you to draw form. An example would be to select red and pink colors to show lighter and darker reds in an illustration. To achieve a full color and value range buy as large a set as you can afford. The softer grades of pastels are ideal for filling in large areas of color, while the harder grades work for drawing lines in more detailed areas.

Paper: Choose relatively large-format paper, because soft pastels do not give sharp colors and create a thicker line. Shapes can be filled with ease on larger paper. Soft pastel colors look great on toned paper—the color of the paper can be used in parts of the drawing. This saves time when illustrating and gives an impression of freshness. White paper is also a good choice for pastel drawing. Textured paper works beautifully with this medium; the pastel adheres to the surface of the paper more readily than it would to a smooth paper.

Strengths: Soft pastel is very good for achieving a strong light and shadow effect on forms. Shapes are easy to depict with this medium.

Drawbacks: The colors smudge and are hard to control due to the lack of a sharp point on the pastel stick. When working with this medium it is hard to keep your hands and the background paper clean. The other drawback is that the finished piece is very fragile and often needs to be framed under glass or sprayed with fixative to avoid smearing the colors.

Ease of use: Moderately difficult—this medium requires deft drawing ability in order to show expertise, and is difficult to control.

△ Pastel on toned paper
The use of toned paper was a time-saver. The blue paper was left without pastel on the drawing of the drapery around the model's waist.

Light and shadow ▷
This drawing shows how white paper can show light and shadow. Dry pastel was applied sparingly, with emphasis on texture. When used as a color accent, pastel provides rich contrast and texture.

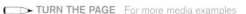

▷ TURN THE PAGE For more media examples

Mixed media

Collage is a good technique to use to understand more about shape. Both the silhouette and the negative space behind the figure can be studied. You can also experiment with more unconventional media such as puff paint, glitter glue, and makeup, to breathe life and fun into your fashion illustrations.

COLLAGE

You will use collage extensively.

Techniques: Collage is perfect for all drawing applications and can be done carefully—with a refined, planned drawing and cut paper, or freely—with the use of life-drawing from a model as the source of the collage, for example.

Buying guide: Save, buy, and accumulate all kinds of paper, including tissue paper, decorative wrapping paper, newspaper and magazine cuttings, photographs, and so on. Fabric scraps and trimmings can also be glued down for collage-making purposes.

Paper: All kinds of paper and other materials are suitable for collage techniques: tracing paper, tissue paper, white drawing paper, watercolor paper, Bristol paper, toned paper, cardboard, shopping bags including the brown grocery type, newspapers and magazines, fabric scraps, and ribbons.

Strengths: A major strength of using collage for fashion illustration is that it is fun to do! It is also the perfect technique to use in order to recycle and use up scraps of materials.

Drawbacks: Collage can be time consuming if you use the approach where each shape is cut from a pattern piece.

Ease of use: Moderate. It's a simple technique but can be hard to make it work convincingly.

Collage drawing
This example of collage drawing used decorative paper for the skirt, tissue paper for the legs, and glitter pens for lipstick accents. The lines were drawn using a piece of charcoal.

Puff paint and glitter glue

Glitter glue and puff paint are sometimes painted onto clothing and can be fun to experiment with when illustrating fashion. The raised surface of the line creates a simple but very effective drawing. These media can be perfect for a portfolio cover design or other graphic presentation, for use in your sketchbook, or for life drawing. The glitter pens also sparkle.

You will use puff paints and glitter glue moderately.

Techniques: Accents; details; portfolio covers; experimental media; accessories; collage drawing.

Buying guide: Buy a set for a wide range of color choices.

Paper: As with gel pens, any format of paper works, and almost any type, including—but not limited to—white drawing paper, watercolor paper, Bristol paper, and toned paper.

Strengths: The three-dimensional, shiny nature of these media make them a superb choice for depicting jewelry and accessories. They give an instant result.

Drawbacks: Puff paint "runs out" and becomes unusable very quickly. Once you have applied them to your work, they are slow to dry.

Ease of use: Easy.

Makeup

The use of makeup as a drawing tool does not require such a stretch of the imagination—this is, after all, fashion illustration, and beauty products make a neat choice to communicate an idea of beauty.

Experimental and fun, makeup is one more medium for you to explore.

You will likely use makeup moderately often as a drawing medium.

Techniques: Accents; details; experimental media; accessories; collage drawing.

Buying guide: To draw with makeup, you need eyeliner for drawing lines and eye shadow colors for shape and soft, shaded effects. Lipstick and nail polish can also add to the drawing, so go a little crazy and bring out the entire makeup kit! Save all free samples and any odd colors that you don't use.

Paper: Drawing with makeup works on all formats of paper and most types. Experiment with tracing paper, white drawing paper, watercolor paper, Bristol paper, and toned paper.

Strengths: Drawing with makeup is fun and experimental.

Drawbacks: Makeup is hard to keep clean and smudge-free once you have applied it to the paper.

Ease of use: Moderate.

△ **Nail polish and eye shadow**
This figure was drawn with eyeliner for the outline contours. Eye shadow was applied over the top of the drawing for texture and color. Nail polish completes the accents on the hair.

◁ **Jewelry and trim**
The raised surface of the paint shows how puff paint creates a decorative surface effect. The paint enhances the depiction of the trim in the neckpiece, and is an example of jewelry drawing with puff paint.

▷ **TURN THE PAGE** For more media examples

What can be said about the beauty of line? That it describes a feeling visually while depicting the illusion of a figure is remarkable. Most people need to work on line, and this chapter will help you evaluate the strengths and weaknesses in your technique. Think powerful, authoritative, and bold when you study line quality. When you enclose a few lines you arrive at a shape. Shapes are easily understood if you think of a silhouette—most fashion illustration is highly involved with a silhouette shape. This chapter helps you understand how the tools of line, shape, and color interact.

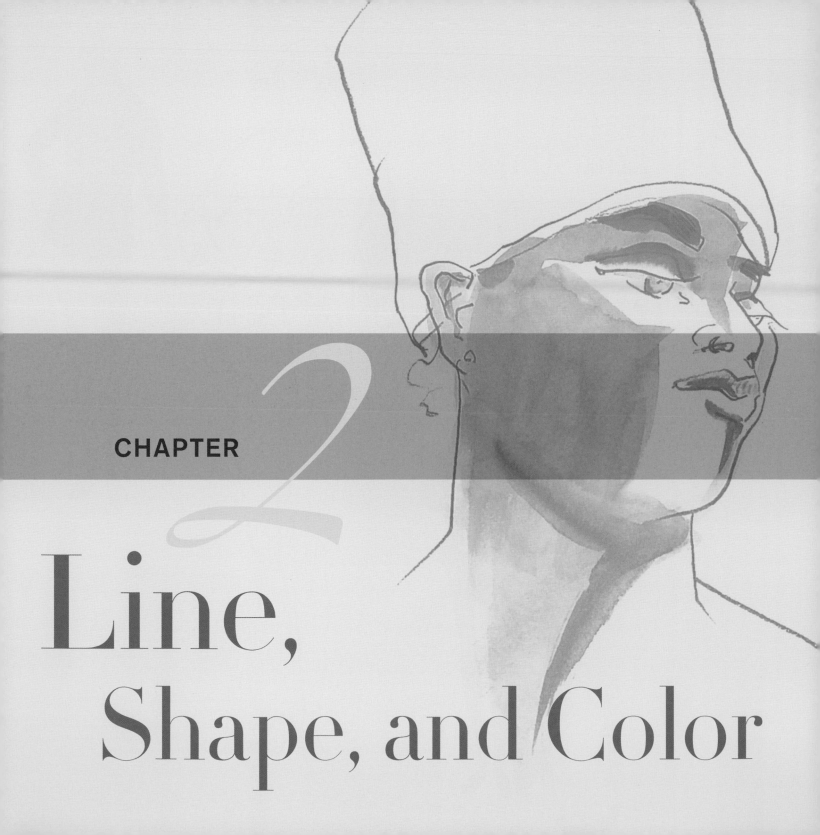

CHAPTER 2

Line, Shape, and Color

TECHNIQUE 8 Line and shape

Line and shape are the two quintessential qualities that define fashion illustration. Minimal lines convey the message with only a few marks. Graphic shapes are used to show a garment's silhouette, the shape of the whole body, light and shadow, or to depict pieces of clothing and body areas.

LINE

Line is to fashion illustration what a sentence is to a writer. Line by line, a fashion illustration becomes a powerful creation and gives detailed information to the viewer about the clothes, as well as the expression and attitude of the model. By using line to communicate precisely what is happening with the clothes, you can simplify your illustration and draw with confidence.

SILHOUETTE

The silhouetted shape communicates both the essential idea of the garment and the model's pose. Does the image show a relaxed figure in pants, or is it a formal dress and a more elegant pose? Does it suggest a loose fit or a tighter line? Shape gives the viewer the answer to these questions; visual communication relies on it.

FLAT SHAPES

Flat shapes are also valuable tools. They can be simple or complex and are key to communicating expression. Combine enough of them and a story emerges. Shapes enhance your illustration and provide the framework for texture and color.

Information types
Compare the information conveyed by these three illustrations: silhouette (far left), line (left), and flat shapes (above).

LIGHT AND SHADOW SHAPES

The form of the figure can be created in more depth and with greater volume when you use light and shadow. When you look at the simple version of what happens with light and shadow, you see two shapes.

Black and white
Here you can see white used for the highlights and black for the shadow area.

Working with value
In this illustration you can see how using light and shadow on form can be a challenge when the clothing values include extremes of lights and darks. The key is to keep the adjacent shapes close in value and not to draw the value steps in too much contrast. Consulting a value chart (below) will help you determine the clothing's shape and color in grayscale.

VALUE CHART

This value chart illustrates a basic value scale. Seeing full color and value contrast in life is an experience that translates into a much smaller range of values in paint. It is only possible to depict around nine to 12 different values in paint. When translating color into value, the base color of the clothing is placed near a value chart and the local color value is assessed. The adjacent colors on the illustration can then be mixed lighter or darker accordingly.

| Value 1 | Value 2 | Value 3 | Value 4 | Value 5 | Value 6 | Value 7 | Value 8 | Value 9 |

Hat   **Pants**   **Hair**   **Skin tone**   **Jacket**

Local color

TECHNIQUE

9 Line quality

To draw well with line is to simplify much of the drawing into a few key marks that have the power to be expressive. Lines that are thin might communicate a fragile, delicate lace effect; while a thick line can be used for leather or bolder denim fabric.

MAKING LINES SAY WHAT YOU WANT

Using line successfully is about studying the subject carefully and translating what you see—and what you want the viewer to see—into a graphic mark. These marks can be varied in both weight and value in order to convey the meaning of anything you want to express in your illustration.

Back view with minimal lines
Lines that show the body in a concise and minimal manner are perfect for fashion illustration. The figure here has a few key lines and these have been selected to show the pose and the figure clearly, while still being stylish and interesting. The weight of the lines varies between wide and thin. You see how even the lines that have been removed are part of the beauty of less being more.

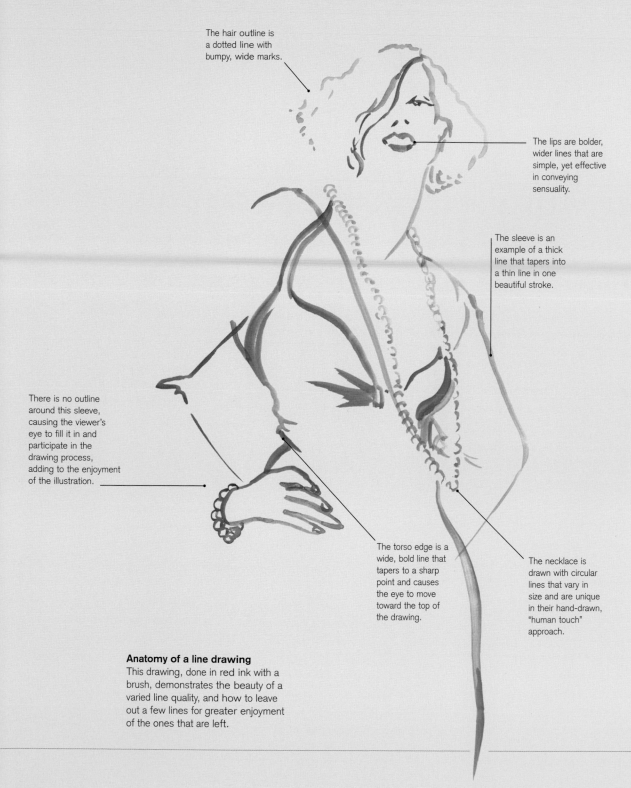

The hair outline is a dotted line with bumpy, wide marks.

The lips are bolder, wider lines that are simple, yet effective in conveying sensuality.

The sleeve is an example of a thick line that tapers into a thin line in one beautiful stroke.

There is no outline around this sleeve, causing the viewer's eye to fill it in and participate in the drawing process, adding to the enjoyment of the illustration.

The torso edge is a wide, bold line that tapers to a sharp point and causes the eye to move toward the top of the drawing.

The necklace is drawn with circular lines that vary in size and are unique in their hand-drawn, "human touch" approach.

Anatomy of a line drawing
This drawing, done in red ink with a brush, demonstrates the beauty of a varied line quality, and how to leave out a few lines for greater enjoyment of the ones that are left.

TECHNIQUE 10 Color and texture

Color may be realistic—matched exactly to lifelike colors—or the color harmony may be expressive and non-realistic to portray a mood. Textures should suggest, not copy, the surface characteristics.

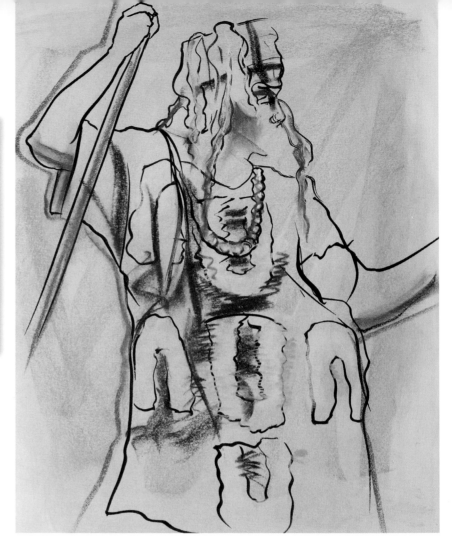

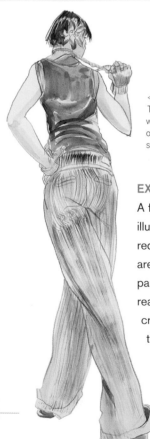

Richly textured fabric ▷
In this African textile illustration, the shirt color is gold, but you can see accents of brown and yellow, which hint at the richness of this textured fabric.

◁ **Corduroy texture**
These pants are richly textured corduroy, created with green, brown, and black. The texture brings out the main tone and shows a lighter and darker side so the pants have volume.

EXPRESSIVE VS. REALISTIC

A fabric swatch glued next to an illustration on a presentation board will require that the colors of the clothing are represented correctly, while other parts of the illustration can be non-realistic. Expressive colors are easy to create and don't require a lot of thought. Good color harmony can be achieved simply by combining colors you find attractive.

You should be aware of color properties: "value" refers to the light and dark properties of a color; "temperature" refers to an evocation by the color of a cool or warm property; and "extension" refers to the amount of each color you use; in general, unequal mixes are more successful.

You can follow the "rules" on how to employ colors to their best advantage or you can choose to be more intuitive. Start making color notebooks. Collect colored scraps of paper and fabric swatches and see what you gravitate toward. After learning how your personal palette is influenced, try using colors that are not so familiar to you. Experimentation is key.

Realistic color is informative and reflects reality. The same scene illustrated with non-realistic color gives a very different feeling. You can illustrate either way—your choices will depend on your objective.

REVEALING TEXTURE

Textures appeal to our sense of touch and add interest and complexity to illustrations. Colors are revealed through lighting, while texture is more apparent to the eye when light shines on form. This is because surfaces, including fabrics and skin tones, either reflect light or absorb it. You will see texture in greater detail at the area on the form where light and shadow meet— so to illustrate a texture successfully, place more emphasis there by lightening the texture on both the highlight and shadow areas nearby.

▽ **Knit texture**
The knit pants on the model are brown, and the thickly textured knit is depicted with gray, brown, and orange. This texture is depicted on the edge where light and shadow shapes meet. The fabrics shown are all absorbing light and have a matte finish. Observe the textures in your illustrations and notice the unique colors that are revealed.

Local and accent colors
These garments (left, right, and above) are full of texture and show the concept of creating vibrant color within a local color form. Note the shirt in the back view (right), where the colors consist of yellow, violet, and green. The shirt has a violet local color, while the other colors add interest to the base color. As a general rule, when creating accents, allow more than three-quarters of the local color to show.

◁ **Texture experiments**
This chart shows experiments in painting textures. Most textures are created with dry brush techniques. Remember to drip, scratch, and layer the paint surface when you explore textures.

▷ **Simple light and shadow shapes**
Notice how all the figures in these illustrations have simple light and shadow shapes. Each of these shapes is distinct and beautifully formed.

MANIPULATING TEXTURE AND COLOR

Play with texturing only one side of the form, such as the highlight area; or use it over the entire form. If a texture is going to appear all over the form, attempt to keep a sense of volume by rendering the sides of the form a little darker in value on the first layer. When you use color to bring out a visual texture, consider using more than one version of the base color. So, if you are painting a red garment, try applying many reds to the main color for greater complexity. Textures that are not smooth generally have multiple color influences. For example, a gray or a brown rock actually contains a myriad of colors; a "brown" rock may contain brown, yellow, and orange, with gold accents; a myriad of colors revealed by light.

1	2	3	4	5	6	7	8	9

Nine values
Although art materials do not replicate the wider range of values that you see in real life, you can translate most color into a simple value. You can easily paint nine values so try this and use it as a basis for understanding how to translate color into value contrast with light on form.

Relative values
The chart shows how all colors at their most vibrant state can be assigned a value. Here, yellow is 3, blue is 7, and red is 6. Each color can be painted in lighter and darker values, as seen in this value scale.

ACCENTS

Try to see more than the local color when looking at a form. An accent is a color—usually selected intuitively—that provides a source of interest when it is placed in the picture. A yellow accent in an orange shirt will bring out the color of the orange. A more unlikely blue accent could also work. Accents are small amounts of color that look interesting—so don't overdo them.

BUILDING LAYERS

When rendering texture, work on getting layers into the illustration. For example, place a ground color down in pastel and overlap with other colors. Use a base color for watercolor and then add colored pencils over the top for texture. Experiment with texture in illustration by using a spatter effect over a ground color, or by dry brushing one color over another one.

◁ **Red light, cool shadow**
The red and blue/green face demonstrates the principle of warm red lights and cool blue/green shadows.

COLOR AND LIGHT TEMPERATURE

The effects of light on form are interesting to study. The color of the light may be warm or cool. When there is a warm light, the shadows will be cool. When a cool light defines the figure, there will be a warm shadow. These principles affect all color rendering for illustrations. For example, if a white garment is lit by a warm highlight, the shadow will be a cooler color. On white fabric a warm light will appear as a pale golden color while the shadow will be blue, and with cool light source a white garment will appear pale blue in the highlight and warmer, orange-toned in the shadow.

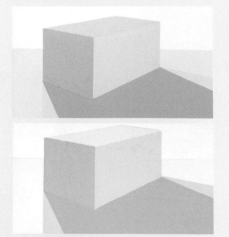

△ **Warm and cool light**
These illustrations of a white cuboid show the effects of warm light and cool light on the highlight and shadow shapes.

△ **Blue/green light, cool shadow**
This model demonstrates warm blue/green and gold light and cool violet shadows.

Skin tones
This figure has a cool shadow on her face and the skin tones are white paper with a more blue shadow.

COLOR AND VALUE MATCHING

The key to getting a good color match with art media is to aim at mixing or creating the color by analyzing its properties. How light is it and what color does it seem? Is it mostly green, and how bright is it? You can mix the color through subtle additions of pigments to lighten, darken, or mute it until you get a close match.

PRACTICING COLOR MATCHING

Paint looks a different color when it is wet, so allow for the value change that can occur as it dries. One way to practice matching colors is to cut swatches of paper out of a magazine and mix up paint to match them. Trial and error will enable you to become more skilled at color matching.

LIGHT EFFECTS AND VALUE CONTRAST

As light hits the form of the body you will see two distinct shapes on the figure. The form will be divided into shapes of light and shadow: the "highlight" and the "shadow shape." Determine the shapes by lighting the model with a spotlight from one side. Experiment with the angle of the light. A good formula is to keep the light shining from above and to the side.

Keeping a simple light and shadow shape is essential for showing volume effectively and developing the form.

▷ **Realistic color matching**
The color in this illustration is a match to original garments. The body and hair colors are also realistic.

▽ **Expressive color**
The color of this model's hair is not a match to her realistic color and the necklace has reflective color accents.

◁ **Swatches**
The magazine swatches (top line) are matched with paint (bottom line). Subtle textures are applied to make the match complete.

Divide each form into two basic shapes of unequal proportion. Then decide on a value and color for every shape in the illustration. There are garment shapes, body shapes, and background shapes. All these shapes will have a distinct local value. For instance, a shirt may be yellow and the main value on it could be 3 on a 9-point value scale. Most paint systems range to fewer values than exist in life, so determine the main value for each shape and then find two more values of each color to show the light and shadow shapes. So, since a black skirt is a local value of nine, the highlight of black is a seven. Each local value has two associated values, and that rule determines the color and value of all forms.

WHITE AND BLACK

Illustrating white and black fabrics presents a particular set of challenges when considering how to show light and shadow through relative value.

WHITE FABRIC

Illustrations of white fabric require a light touch with value. The garments must be created with values that illustrate light and shadow shapes, but the dark value on white is only around two or three. All white fabric rendering on white paper needs to show up. It can be effective to draw a shape around the figure to make it stand out more. Another good technique for rendering white garments is to use a toned paper. The paper color you select for illustrating a white garment should have a value of three or four. Illustrate the garment by letting the paper color be the shadow shape, and only rendering the highlight.

▷ **White on cream**
This example of a white dress on a cream colored paper illustrates the highlight shape with white gouache while the shadow shape is formed by the paper color.

◁ **Contour lines**
This illustration of white fabric shows the way to create shadow shapes without making the value too dark. The white fabric is clearly white and the contour lines around the garment shape make the garment stand out against the white background paper.

▭▷ **TURN THE PAGE** For more color and texture examples

BLACK FABRIC

When black fabric is rendered it is difficult to see the seams and details over the top. One way to remedy this is to draw the shape of the black garment and use a lighter color to add the details over the top of the main shape. The other way is to gradually gradate the black color from value five to value nine over a small area of the garment. This method requires that at least three-quarters of the area of the garment is rendered in black. In this way the fabric has a local color of black and cannot be confused with gray fabric. A black pencil line over the layer of color is a good way to clarify the shape and illustrate the full value range. Try drawing a black line around the shape and leaving a small white space between the line and the shape. This uses the space as a guide to the shape's contours and gives a graphic look.

▷ **Pencil details**
This male figure has a black jacket illustrated with black watercolor applied to the shape; black pencil lines show the details of the collar and the seams.

◁ **Blue undertone**
The black pants on this figure have an undertone of blue. The color is a rich combination of dark blue and black with texture applied on top to show a lighter gray value on the knee area.

▷ **Watercolor wash**
The black coat has pattern on top and the first layer is a watercolor wash with gradations of lighter value.

▷ **Black and white rendering**
This illustration shows both black and white fabric rendering. The skirt has a small portion that is left white to show a light shape; however it is clearly black because most of the shape is black. The skirt is outlined with black pencil and has a small amount of white paper showing between the line and the skirt shape. There is one transitional gray shape between the black and white areas, making the garment appear to have dimension and form. The white shirt is white paper and has a pale gray value number two shadow shape. Notice how effectively the leg contour line colors bring out the form of the body. The fur wrap is created with a black line and texture, while the shape and contour line show a larger white space between these two areas.

▷ **White lines**
This figure has white lines defining folds and the edge of the skirt.

SOLID COLOR FABRICS

With all solid color garments, look for the opportunity to create a light and dark value of the color. Remember to check your value pattern, and if the local color is a value number five then don't make the shadow color darker than a value number seven. If the fabric is reflective, you can render more values in the solid color fabric illustration.

Work on avoiding rendering the local color as a boring color that is isolated in the croquis. Avoid this by illustrating the local color in another area of the illustration to draw the eye to a repetition of color. So, if a blue skirt is rendered, then paint the eye shadow in blue or repeat blue on the shoes or nail color. The eye should find a way through the illustration, and repeating a color will create this path.

△ ▷ **Local colors**
The colors are clearly stated and in each case you can see the local color. In some fabrics there will be more shine in the surface texture.

Yes, there is a body underneath those clothes. All fashion illustrators know this and understand how fundamentally important the figure is to fashion drawing. In this chapter, feet, hands, the face, and arms and legs will be revealed to you as well as information about how to balance a standing figure. The consistent component to most good fashion illustration is the solid drawing of the body. The attitude of the figure will be explored so you can perfect the creation of the center front and back lines on the figure as well as depict excellent expression through "pushing" the pose.

CHAPTER 3

The Fashion Figure

Fashion proportions

Proportion guidelines exist to help the illustrator develop a figure that shows clothes to the best advantage. Fashion proportions are stylized and generally favor the taller, leaner figure—but there are exceptions to this. The following guidelines can be adjusted to suit your personal taste.

Creating a figure

The study of proportions is about learning how to relate one area of the drawing to another so that all parts create a solid whole. Fashion models are proportioned in a specific way and are uniquely suited to wearing almost any cut and style of clothing. Clothes look beautiful on a fashion model's body and the proportional standard that an illustrator draws is fixed in part by the typical fashion model's proportions. Create proportions and exaggerate body angles according to your needs. There is great flexibility in fashion illustration proportions. The type of garment being illustrated, the personal preference of the individual artist, and the particular trend of the moment will all be factors determining how you proportion your figure.

Thirds

One stylized standard of proportions in a fashion figure is to use "thirds." One third of the body consists of the top of the head to the waist. The waist to the knees makes up another third. The final third is the area between the knees and the soles of the feet. This makes for a tall figure, somewhat

Figure comparison

These two figures are proportioned the same in length, and have slim, fit figures. The male figure is depicted with more angularity while the female figure is curved.

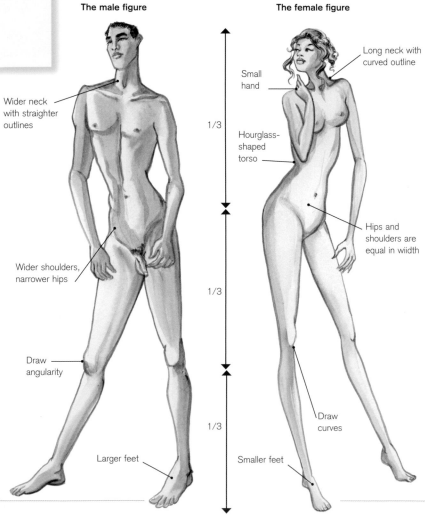

The male figure

Wider neck with straighter outlines

Wider shoulders, narrower hips

Draw angularity

Larger feet

The female figure

Long neck with curved outline

Small hand

Hourglass-shaped torso

Hips and shoulders are equal in wiidth

Draw curves

Smaller feet

1/3

1/3

1/3

similar to drawing a realistic representation of a typical fashion model. Following this formula, most fashion illustrations will work well.

The male and female fashion figure proportions are identical in length for this standard. The figures of both genders have a small head in relation to the body. Both figures will have more length in the upper torso, and a smaller lower torso—also called the "pelvic box." In both the male and female figures, the legs will be shorter in the upper leg length and longer in the lower leg length.

Emphasizing gender differences

The main differences when illustrating the genders are to create more width in a male figure's neck, as well as wider shoulders, slim hips and waist, larger hands, and larger feet. A female figure will have a curved, slender neck with narrow shoulders, slim hips and waist, smaller hands, and delicate feet. The trick in illustrating the gender differences is to draw strong curves for the female figure and angles for the male figure.

THE CHANGING FIGURE

Many fashion illustrations are stylized a lot, while others use more realistic proportions and much less elongation. Proportional guidelines may apply to a particular era of clothing. For example, in the 1920s the fashion figure was long and lean. The 1960s figure was similar—but showed more of the leg and knee. The 1950s era gave the fashion illustrator a demand for a longer torso, to make the waist a good place to draw a belt. As styles of clothing change, proportional standards change. A good guideline is to go with the style and trend of the moment and use proportions that best communicate the particular style of clothing.

Slight adjustments
These two male models (left) are almost the same height, though the figure on the left is slightly shorter. When proportioning a figure, you can decide the degree of exaggeration you would like to use; sometimes even a slight adjustment can give a more elegant appearance to the clothing.

Proportional manipulation
In the illustrations on the right, one model is very tall and the other one is shorter. Observe the way one model appears sleek and the other one is average-looking. If an illustration is drawn realistically and the model is short, you may get a good drawing but the clothing is likely to look less flattering. These drawings illustrate the concept of proportional manipulation.

TECHNIQUE 12
The torso

The torso is a complicated form composed of two areas; the upper torso is longer than the lower. The two are hinged at the waist and movement occurs there. The large range of motion in the torso and its ability to twist and turn is what gives a fashion illustration much of its power. The side, backward, and forward bending movements all create opportunities for more dynamic and believable drawing.

Breaking the torso down

The upper torso includes the shoulders—which can move independently of each other—and the hips—which are a solid form. The hip bones are constructed in such a way that one side moves upward while the opposite side moves down. You will need to study the shoulder angles, width, and shape in order to draw with authority.

The lower torso includes the pelvic bones. The pelvic area can be thought of as a box, and drawn with side and front planes. This box structure helps illustrate the way clothing curves around the figure in perspective. The box is a non-realistic form that is not included in a finished illustration, but helps in the understanding of the underlying structure. The box is angled backward more on the female figure. A side viewpoint of a male figure would show a vertical pelvis.

In drawing the torso, the figure is usually depicted as two forms, hinged at the waist. The waist allows the upper torso to move, while the lower remains fixed and rigid. Drawing the torso from all four sides will enhance your understanding of it.

Symmetry or motion
These three torso views were drawn at eye level. The symmetrical view shows an even shoulder, waist, and hip alignment, while the figure next to it is an asymmetrical pose with the shoulders higher on one side.

Pelvic box

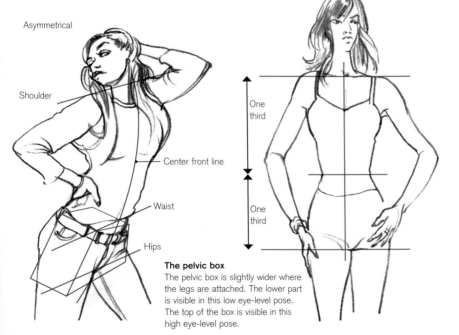

Asymmetrical

Symmetrical

Shoulder

Center front line

Waist

Hips

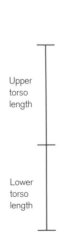
One third

One third

The pelvic box
The pelvic box is slightly wider where the legs are attached. The lower part is visible in this low eye-level pose. The top of the box is visible in this high eye-level pose.

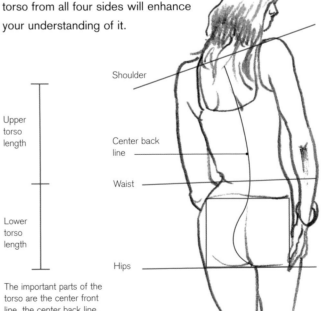

Shoulder

Upper torso length

Lower torso length

Center back line

Waist

Hips

The important parts of the torso are the center front line, the center back line, and the waist area.

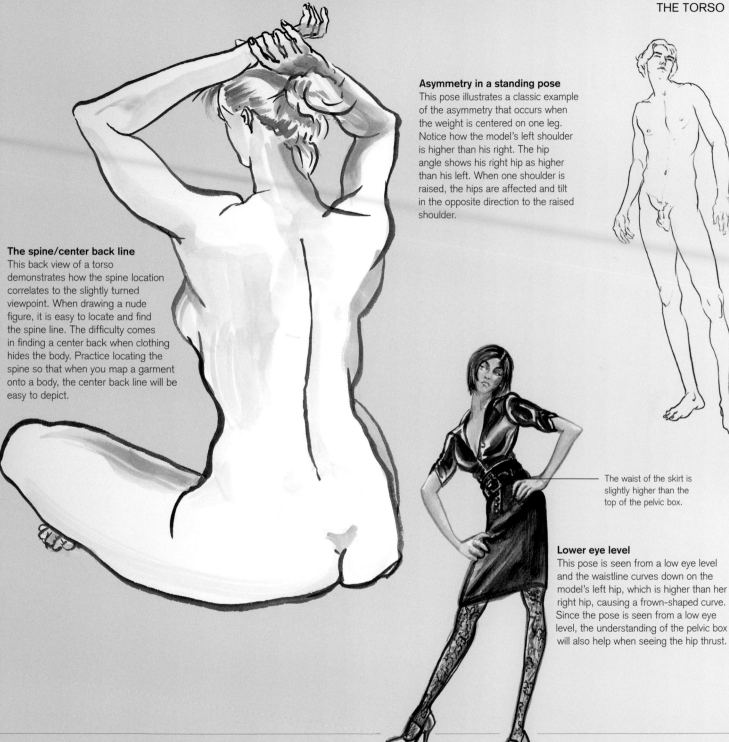

Asymmetry in a standing pose
This pose illustrates a classic example of the asymmetry that occurs when the weight is centered on one leg. Notice how the model's left shoulder is higher than his right. The hip angle shows his right hip as higher than his left. When one shoulder is raised, the hips are affected and tilt in the opposite direction to the raised shoulder.

The spine/center back line
This back view of a torso demonstrates how the spine location correlates to the slightly turned viewpoint. When drawing a nude figure, it is easy to locate and find the spine line. The difficulty comes in finding a center back when clothing hides the body. Practice locating the spine so that when you map a garment onto a body, the center back line will be easy to depict.

The waist of the skirt is slightly higher than the top of the pelvic box.

Lower eye level
This pose is seen from a low eye level and the waistline curves down on the model's left hip, which is higher than her right hip, causing a frown-shaped curve. Since the pose is seen from a low eye level, the understanding of the pelvic box will also help when seeing the hip thrust.

TECHNIQUE
Legs

Legs are a strong feature of fashion illustrations. Most garments look good on a model in a dynamic walking pose. Here, helpful ideas about how to draw the legs from all angles are explored through a look at the anatomy and shape of this important body form. As with all other parts of the body, the proportions of a "typical" leg are exaggerated in fashion illustration to achieve a particular look and show the clothes to their best advantage.

Leg structure

The legs are capable of a great deal of motion. As you draw them, observe the knee and how it is structured. Notice how it is higher at the back of the leg than in front. To draw the leg, you need to understand the directional angle of the form and then draw in the correct curves. The motion of the leg is determined by the bend in the knee. Dividing the leg into halves at the knee produces the proportions of the leg in a standing pose. If you need a walking pose, the legs will vary in length on the upper and lower parts—and the eye level of the viewer will determine which part should be longer.

The fashion leg

The main key to a "fashion leg" is to make the upper leg—from the top to the knee—shorter than the lower leg—from the knee to the foot. This creates a beautiful line with graceful proportions. The calf muscle must be drawn in the correct area; be careful not to draw the curve too high. Work to get enough width in the knee area. The ankle is a transitional point, where you can show graceful form between the leg and foot.

Overlapping forms
This figure demonstrates the way that both the arms and the legs show overlapping forms when the viewpoint creates a foreshortened figure. When you are drawing, remind yourself which elements are closer and which are farther away to give you an idea of how to overlap the contour lines.

WALKING POSES

Legs in motion are the most difficult to draw. The best approach is to observe for yourself what is aesthetically pleasing. Visual attractiveness in an illustration could simply be a matter of creating uneven and therefore less static shapes. Because visual interest has a lot to do with design, you can think about how to arrange the forms, and always trust your eye over a fixed set of rules. Generally, though, an overlapping arrangement of legs works better than legs that are spread apart. Create poses that have a balance of lengths and widths. Remember that in all walking poses both legs will be bent to some extent.

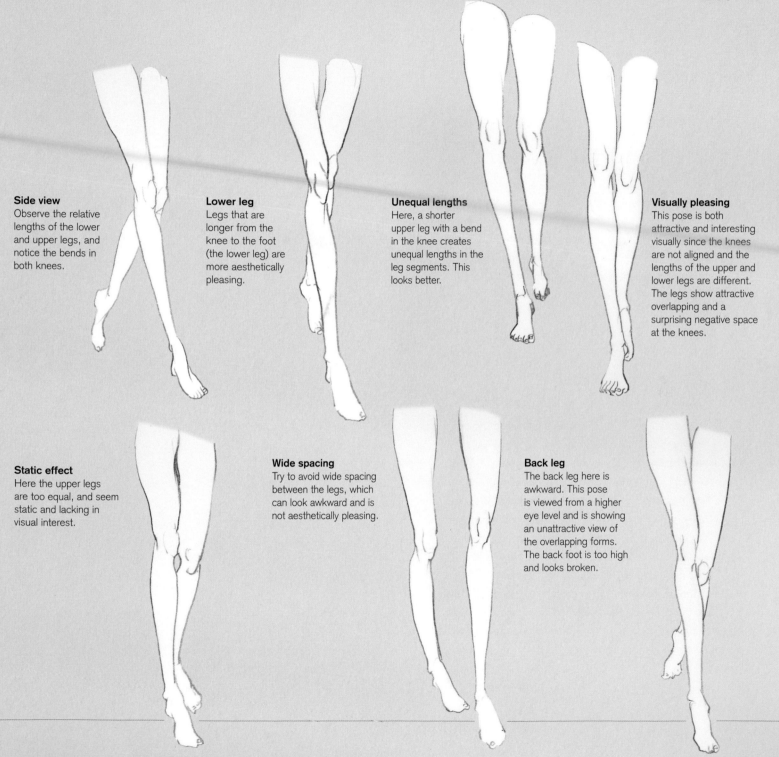

Side view
Observe the relative lengths of the lower and upper legs, and notice the bends in both knees.

Lower leg
Legs that are longer from the knee to the foot (the lower leg) are more aesthetically pleasing.

Unequal lengths
Here, a shorter upper leg with a bend in the knee creates unequal lengths in the leg segments. This looks better.

Visually pleasing
This pose is both attractive and interesting visually since the knees are not aligned and the lengths of the upper and lower legs are different. The legs show attractive overlapping and a surprising negative space at the knees.

Static effect
Here the upper legs are too equal, and seem static and lacking in visual interest.

Wide spacing
Try to avoid wide spacing between the legs, which can look awkward and is not aesthetically pleasing.

Back leg
The back leg here is awkward. This pose is viewed from a higher eye level and is showing an unattractive view of the overlapping forms. The back foot is too high and looks broken.

TECHNIQUE 14
Arms

When you draw the arms on your fashion figures, be sure to make them the correct length. If you draw the arms too short, it can make the clothing seem to fit badly. An arm that hangs straight down to the side with no bend in the elbow should usually be proportioned to hang to the middle of the upper leg.

Drawing arms

To draw an arm well, it is essential to understand foreshortened form. Many views of arms show the arm bending and the upper and lower parts overlapping. A foreshortened arm looks wider than an arm that is hanging straight down to the side of the body. Observe where the elbow falls and notice that the inner arm is located in a higher position than the outer elbow. Look for the directional angle of the arm, and ask yourself before drawing it if it is more diagonal, has a bend in the elbow, or hangs straight on the pose you have selected. You can vastly improve the quality of your fashion illustrations through a careful study of arms.

Arm extension
The angles of both arms, as seen in this pose, show how difficult the shapes of this complicated form are. Remember to draw the directional angles with a flowing curve. Although there are many curves and complexities in the structure of the figure, the main idea is to show the limbs, including the legs, moving in a particular direction while at the same time seeking to capture the subtle overlapping of the forms.

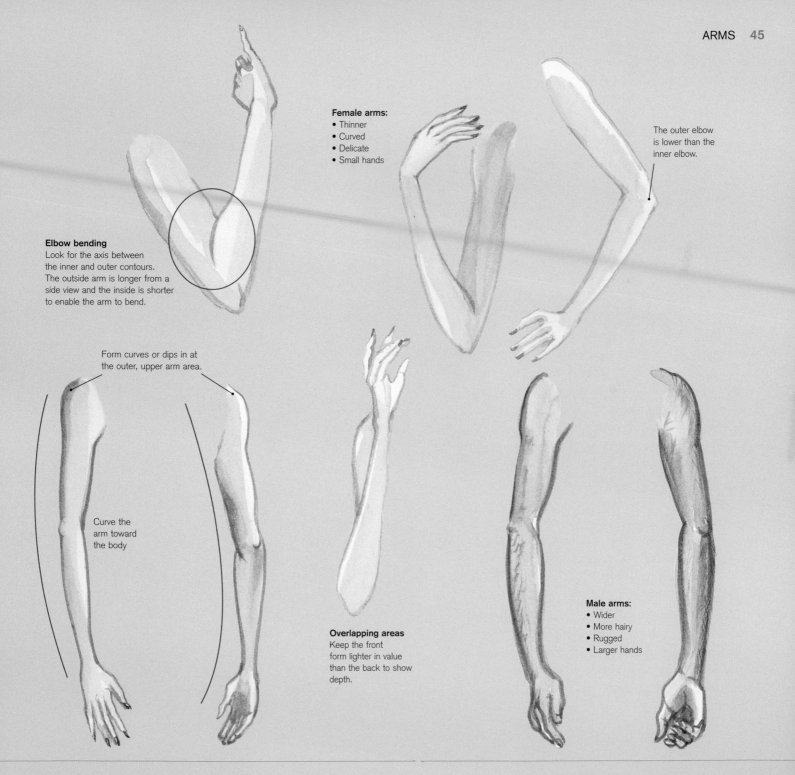

Female arms:
- Thinner
- Curved
- Delicate
- Small hands

The outer elbow is lower than the inner elbow.

Elbow bending
Look for the axis between the inner and outer contours. The outside arm is longer from a side view and the inside is shorter to enable the arm to bend.

Form curves or dips in at the outer, upper arm area.

Curve the arm toward the body

Overlapping areas
Keep the front form lighter in value than the back to show depth.

Male arms:
- Wider
- More hairy
- Rugged
- Larger hands

TURN THE PAGE For hands and feet

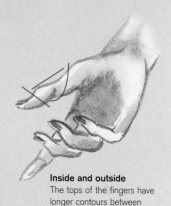

Inside and outside
The tops of the fingers have longer contours between knuckles than the undersides.

Hands and feet

A fashion hand should be long and tapered in the fingers; all lines should be smooth and continuous. Hands usually rest on the hips or hang to the sides. Feet are often in heels, causing a diagonal directional angle on the foot shape.

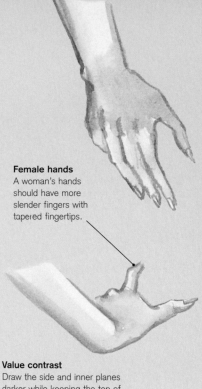

Female hands
A woman's hands should have more slender fingers with tapered fingertips.

Drawing hands

Good hand drawing relies on a careful observational study of details and an understanding of key areas. These include the transition area of the wrist, the place where motion occurs. Extend the hand through the wrist and arm as you draw. You need to consider hand poses carefully to achieve consistency with the proportions of the rest of the body. The complicated forms of the fingers from a foreshortened viewpoint can be an opportunity to draw overlapping shapes and suggest depth.

Look at the negative space between the fingers to help you draw the hand shape. Also note that the fingers are longer on top than underneath to allow for bending inward.

Gender differences

The gender differences between the male and female hands include the idea of drawing the male hands larger and more angular (as for the torso, see page 40). Male fingers are squarer and thicker, while female fingers are thinner and more tapered at the fingertips.

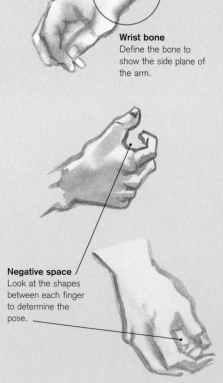

Male hands

Wrist bone
Define the bone to show the side plane of the arm.

Negative space
Look at the shapes between each finger to determine the pose.

Value contrast
Draw the side and inner planes darker while keeping the top of the fingers lighter.

Details
Include specific details like rings and fingernails so the hand doesn't look like a glove.

Drawing feet

Fashion feet are long and slender. The key to good drawing of feet is to see where the leg stops and the foot starts, and draw attractive curves at the ankle. Toes are the details, while the foot itself is a wedge-shaped form. Look closely at the ankle, the overlapping planes, and the foot shape. Draw all the angles with a sense of attractive curving from the leg, through the ankle, to the foot. Observe where the leg ends, and look at the arch of the foot. Also study the anklebone to see which side is higher and which side is lower.

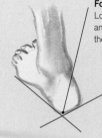

Foot angle
Look at the directional foot angle and determine where the heel is placed.

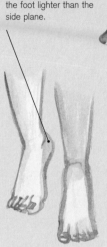

Shading
Work on the directional planes of the foot arch through shading, and leave the top of the foot lighter than the side plane.

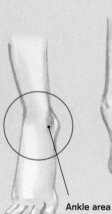

Ankle area
There is a plane change between the leg and the foot at the ankle. Work on seeing this form and use overlapping outline and color to depict the arch of the foot.

Shading
Work on the directional planes of the foot arch through shading, and leave the top of the foot lighter than the side plane.

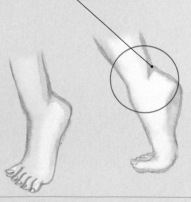

Axis
The inward curve on the top of the foot is mirrored by the arch on the sole of the foot.

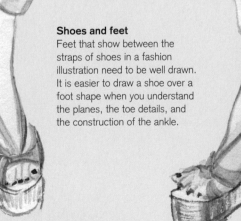

Shoes and feet
Feet that show between the straps of shoes in a fashion illustration need to be well drawn. It is easier to draw a shoe over a foot shape when you understand the planes, the toe details, and the construction of the ankle.

 TURN THE PAGE For croquis figure development

TECHNIQUE 16
Croquis figure development

The development of a croquis figure (a basic, eight-head high fashion figure) is easier if you use a proportional guide. Place the tracing paper over the guide and draw a pose on top of the guidelines to create a figure with the proportions you want. You can make a guide using eight heads, nine heads, or ten heads; the proportions are up to you. The guide is based upon using a "head" as one unit of measurement. The waist falls at three heads, the knees at six heads and the bottom of the feet at nine heads. In this way, the figure is divided into thirds.

HEAD RULE

The gray rule on the edge of the right-hand page (opposite), shows how the figure is divided into heads.

Proportion guide

The drawing on the right shows the key areas that you need to consider when drawing the whole figure.

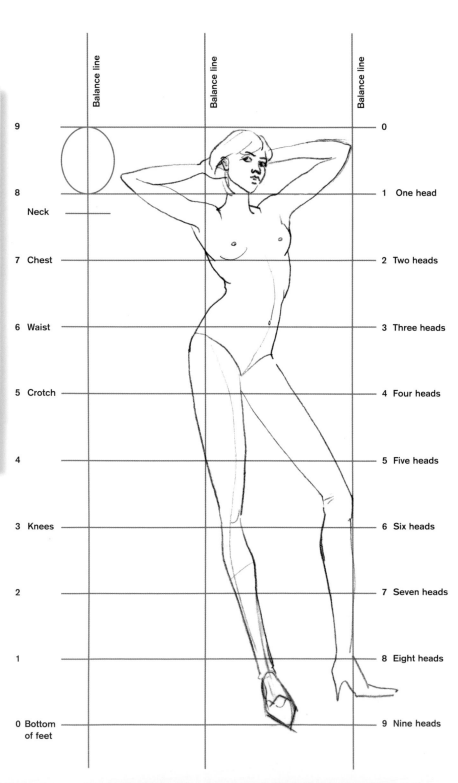

Balance line   Balance line   Balance line

9

8

Neck

7 Chest

6 Waist

5 Crotch

4

3 Knees

2

1

0 Bottom of feet

0
1 One head
2 Two heads
3 Three heads
4 Four heads
5 Five heads
6 Six heads
7 Seven heads
8 Eight heads
9 Nine heads

From rough to finish

This case study shows how to develop a croquis figure. The first step is to find reference that is close to the pose you want to draw. The example shown here uses a photo from a magazine. Redraw this pose using the proportion guide and a piece of tracing paper. When the figure is complete, draw a second tracing paper overlay of the clothing shapes over the body. Then transfer the lines of the sketch to a piece of paper using a lightbox, and color the croquis with your preferred media.

1 Refine the figure and develop a croquis pose. Don't add clothing to this figure because you will design around the body after the figure is completed.

2 Draw the clothing over the croquis.

3 Transfer the drawing and then illustrate and render with your chosen color media.

▭▷ **TURN THE PAGE** For more croquis figure development

The importance of the pose

The pose needs to match the garment you wish to illustrate. This is an example of a 1950s-inspired dress. Notice that the pose is developed to show a flirty attitude and hairstyle typical of the era.

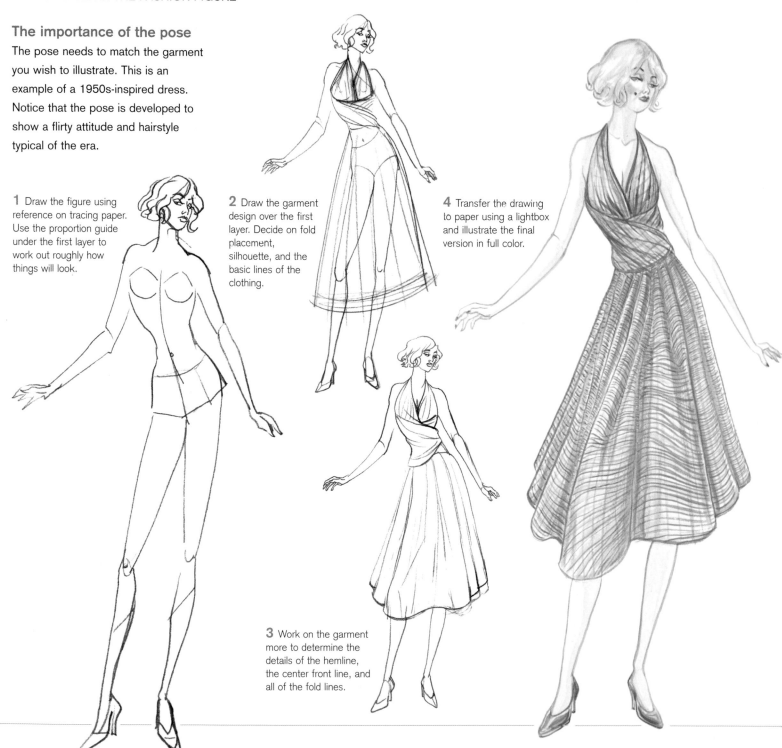

1 Draw the figure using reference on tracing paper. Use the proportion guide under the first layer to work out roughly how things will look.

2 Draw the garment design over the first layer. Decide on fold placement, silhouette, and the basic lines of the clothing.

3 Work on the garment more to determine the details of the hemline, the center front line, and all of the fold lines.

4 Transfer the drawing to paper using a lightbox and illustrate the final version in full color.

Using the same pose with variations

When you have developed a pose, you can use it for more than one illustration. In this example, there are two finished illustrations. One version features a model in a pose with both hands on her hips and the other version shows one arm resting against her side. Look at the difference in attitude and mood of the two figures. Not much was changed in the basic pose, yet the croquis are completely different in expression.

The head
The hairstyle and head can easily change on a croquis figure.

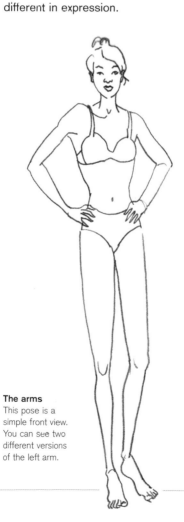

The arms
This pose is a simple front view. You can see two different versions of the left arm.

The croquis
The main pose and figure can be altered to include two different versions of the rough. Here you can see two different heads, one body and foot relationship, and the two different versions of the model's left arm and hand.

▷ TURN THE PAGE For the figure

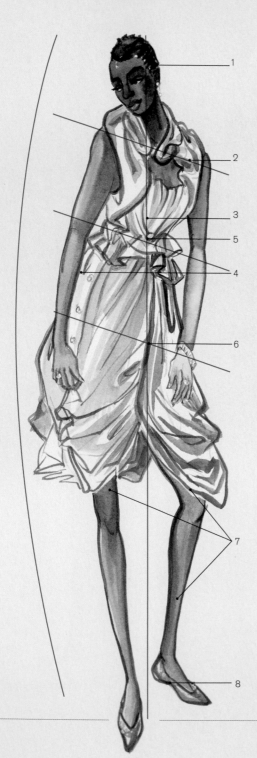

The figure

The figure can be posed in an infinite number of ways. If you understand structure areas that seem to be essential in establishing the pose, you can illustrate the body with greater authority.

Body motion and action

The main idea is to look for how a hip might thrust out more than any other body point. This body motion is a way to determine which side of the figure to draw first. If you draw the hip thrust, you can exaggerate it and then control the width of the body. In this way, you can quickly achieve an expressive drawing with good proportional accuracy.

1. Head angle
Look to see if the model is tipping her head down and watch the top of the head for the angle.

2. Shoulder relationship
Observe the angle of the shoulders and find out which one is higher.

3. Body balance line
Look for the base of the neck and the heel of the supporting leg to determine how to balance the body.

4. The hip thrust
This common fashion pose is drawn by exaggerating the side where the hip is thrusting, and then aligning the rest of the body with this point.

5. Waist/leg relationship
The weight of the body is on the model's right leg and there is no bend in the knee, so the waist reflects the leg action.

6. Hip/leg relationship
The hip angle is often determined by the legs, so watch the pose for which leg has a bend in the knee and which leg is straight. If a leg is straight, the hip will usually be higher on that side.

7. Leg directional angle
Is the leg at a diagonal directional angle or is it straight? When there is a hip thrust, as here, the weighted leg will often move in a diagonal line to balance the body.

8. Feet angle
Look at the bottom of the shoe to determine the foot angle.

Key structure areas
The drawing on the left shows the key areas that you need to consider when drawing the whole figure.

HEM CURVES

As a quick guide, remember:

view from above = hem curves like a smile;

view from below = hem curves like a frown.

Eye level

On a lower eye-level pose, you will see the hemline appear to curve downward at the sides. Think about where your eye level is as you draw a pose in order to see how elements of clothing or clothing lines curve around the form of the figure. On straight eye-level poses, you will see the curves of the hem and the neckline form less exaggerated curves. The hem in this position will follow the hip angle and curve toward the hip thrust, and you will see a higher hem on the hip thrusting side.

Hem following hip thrust
This pose is a good example of a hip thrust and a straight-on eye level. The hem is higher on the model's left side, matching the supporting leg and pelvic box thrust.

Downward-curving hem
Observe the hem of this coat and you will see how the low eye level is depicted through an understanding of how the ellipse of the whole hem curves downward at the sides.

▭▷ **TURN THE PAGE** For more on the figure

Exaggeration

The poses that you create can be developed to show more expression through the use of exaggeration. The trick is to exaggerate with knowledge of what to push and how far to go with the exaggeration. In order to think about how a figure can be manipulated to show greater expression, you need to understand the places on the body where the form is able to bend or stretch. These areas include the connection points, or joints, on the figure. For example, the neck is a connection point between the head and the torso.

This is a place to express attitude. The shoulders can be pushed up or down, and the relationship between the two shoulders is often the main place to refine the figure and exaggerate the pose. The connection of the upper and lower torsos at the waist is the place to really push the rotation of the body, as well as the front, side, and back bend poses. The legs can be placed under the pose to balance the body as you manipulate these areas.

The head
The chin is looking down in both poses and the neck is stretched forward.

The shoulders
Notice how the exaggerated body has a higher right shoulder than in the original pose.

Torso directional angle
Notice the body thrust and how the original pose is slightly diagonal while the exaggerated pose shows the torso to be extended in a more extreme diagonal position.

Negative space
The legs have more space between them in the exaggerated pose.

Original pose

Exaggerated pose

Finding the body

When a garment covers most of the body and you see only a little of the figure underneath, you will have to look for clues to locate the center front line, the waistline, and all other "hidden" parts of the body. If you know how to look for the pelvic box and the main angles of the figure, it will be easier to discover what is happening to that figure under the clothes. Not all of these lines and points will be visible, depending on the pose. Finding one main point or the relationship between two points can show you enough of what you need to continue to draw the pose and get the figure established.

The center front line
In this pose the center front is defined by the wrapped neck opening and the v-shaped overlap under the neck. On a nude figure, the pit of the neck is the key point for the location of the start of the center front line.

The pelvic box
Looking at the drape in this garment, we can find the pose hip tilt and draw this hip angle.

The shoulder line
This is found by looking at where the sweater curves on each shoulder and lining up the top part of this curve.

Negative space
Look for the background space between the arm and the hip, showing the pelvic box tilt.

The body balance line
This can be found by seeing where the neckline and the foot of the supporting leg are located.

The legs
Look at the fact that one leg has a bend in the knee and one is a straight leg. Usually this indicates that the hip is higher on the straight leg side and lower on the bent knee side.

THE FIGURE UNDER CLOTHING

This pose is a good example of the difficulty in finding out what is happening to the body under bulky clothing. The slight amount of upper leg and pants that show behind the sweater is a clue to the pose, since this information tells you that there is a bend in one knee and a straight leg. This gives you another clue—a straight leg and bent knee causes a hip relationship where the hip is thrust to one side and the shoulders tilt more to follow this stance. We can discover that the pit of the neck is underneath the foot, and this is a clue to the pose and body balance. The torso is not showing, so the knowledge of it is based on checking the negative space between the left arm and back to see the hip tilt. There are always clues to help you find the pose and draw the clothing over the body.

Interacting curves

The body forms are interconnected in s-shaped curves, backward s-curves, and c-shaped curves. This is evident in standing nude poses as well as in the individual body forms of the legs and arms. For a more rhythmic figure you can often exaggerate the s-curves, and this is best done in a concept known as "follow-through of the line." Draw the combined curves by thinking of a line running down the center of the form and deciding the direction this line would take if there were a combination of directional angles that curved instead of forming a straight line.

Drawing curves

To complete a more fluid and beautifully formed figure, study the concept of curved directional lines by drawing a single form, seeing where the direction of this form goes, and then curving the angle of the direction to one side. To determine if the line moves one way or another, look at the main direction of the form and try drawing it with one curve or another and see which works best.

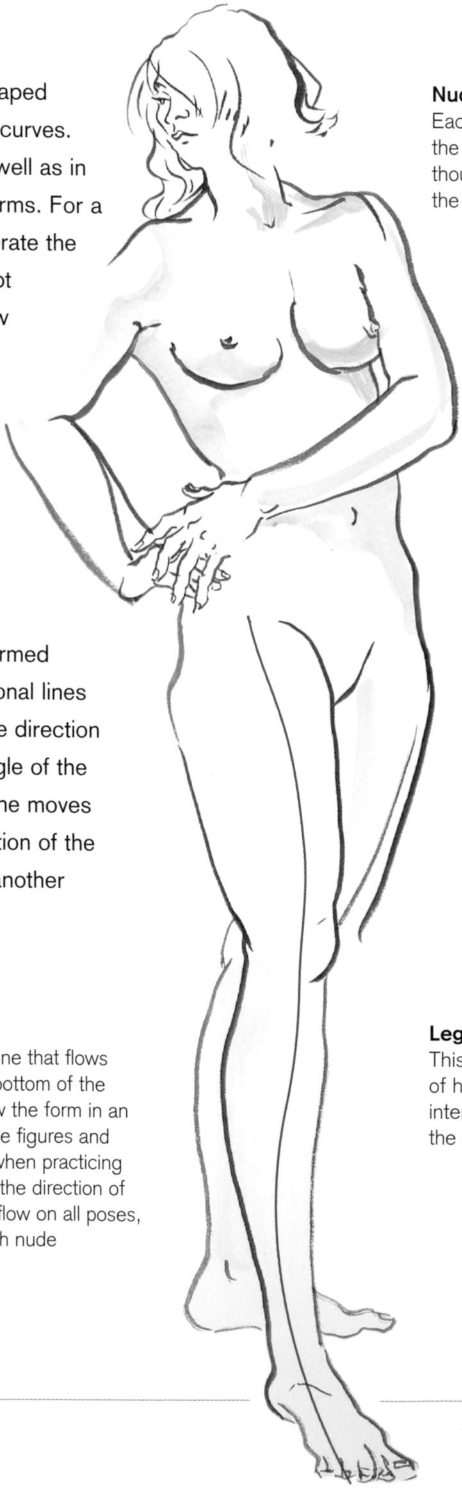

Nude and clothed figures
Each figure shows a curve and the forms flow together even though the clothing often covers the figure.

Flow of line
Draw the body as a continuous line that flows from the top of the head to the bottom of the foot. This will enable you to show the form in an attractive and rhythmic way. Nude figures and standing poses are best to use when practicing drawing by following through on the direction of the line, but curves interact and flow on all poses, including sitting and standing with nude or clothed figures.

Leg curve
This line is a good example of how the forms of the body interact and form curves in the big picture of the form.

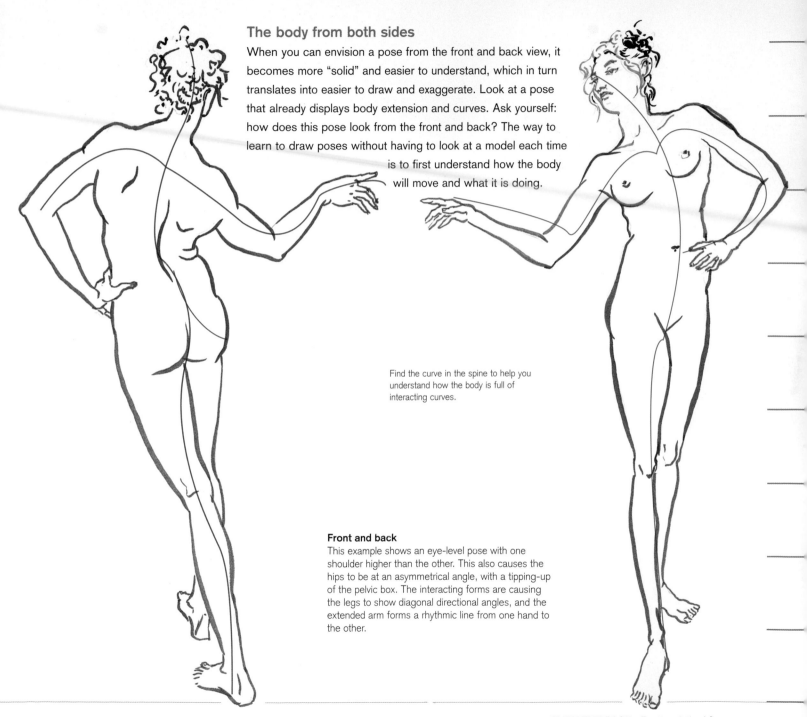

The body from both sides

When you can envision a pose from the front and back view, it becomes more "solid" and easier to understand, which in turn translates into easier to draw and exaggerate. Look at a pose that already displays body extension and curves. Ask yourself: how does this pose look from the front and back? The way to learn to draw poses without having to look at a model each time is to first understand how the body will move and what it is doing.

Find the curve in the spine to help you understand how the body is full of interacting curves.

Front and back
This example shows an eye-level pose with one shoulder higher than the other. This also causes the hips to be at an asymmetrical angle, with a tipping-up of the pelvic box. The interacting forms are causing the legs to show diagonal directional angles, and the extended arm forms a rhythmic line from one hand to the other.

✏️ **TURN THE PAGE** For the clothed figure

TECHNIQUE 18

The clothed figure

When you create a fashion illustration, the body and the pose must be clearly established. Starting with a nude, and progressing by drawing clothed figures after you understand the nude, is a good formula for successfully achieving the illusion of form and depth in your illustrations.

Remembering the body

Clothing obscures the body, and it is easy to get lost in drawing clothing shapes and forgetting about the figure under the clothing. There are ways to avoid this trap, and on the following pages you can find out how to see clothing as forms that are not flat. The volume of clothing, with convincing garment forms, can enhance depth, space, solidity, and give a pleasing bulk to the body. Remember, though, that the figure is the main structure and the clothing is placed over this framework. You can easily improve your fashion illustrations by drawing clothing that fits over a "solid" figure.

Comparison of a clothed and nude figure
Notice how important a strong knowledge of figure drawing is in helping you draw clothing. Clothes often hide the center front line, the waist, and the hip thrust, so you have to see through to the body as you design the clothes for a full and convincing form.

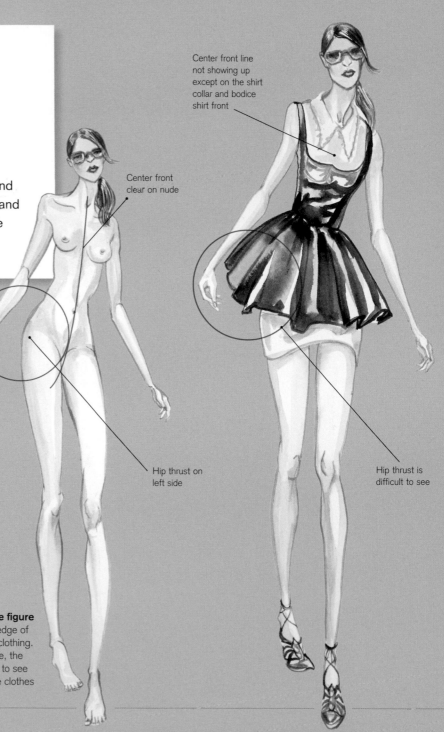

Center front line not showing up except on the shirt collar and bodice shirt front

Center front clear on nude

Hip thrust on left side

Hip thrust is difficult to see

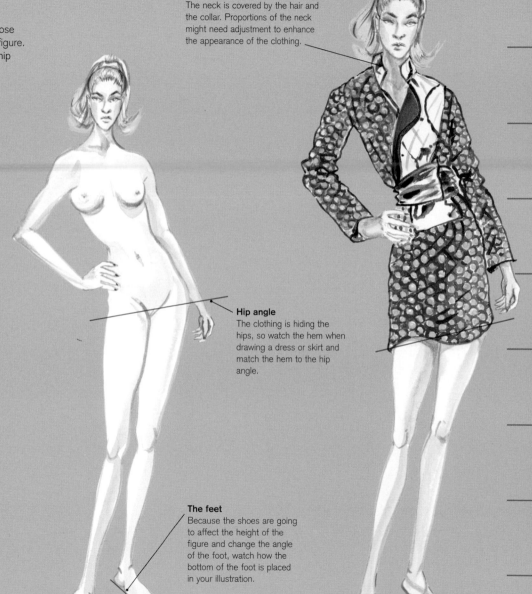

The pose
The angles of the pose are clear in a nude figure. This pose shows a hip thrust to one side.

Hair and collar
The neck is covered by the hair and the collar. Proportions of the neck might need adjustment to enhance the appearance of the clothing.

3D clothing

The way to think about illustrating clothing over the form of the body is to draw the clothing as if it were three-dimensional. This is easy to do when you realize that the clothing is not "painted" onto a figure like a tattoo. So, the body angles will affect the hemline where the model is wearing a skirt. The sleeves of a jacket will form folds when the model bends an arm to place a hand on the hip. If the hair is covering the neck, watch the length of it and get the directional angle established by seeing the way the head is tilted. Don't allow the clothing to cause you to "lose" the pose and the body under it. When you study the illustration process you will see you have layers. The figure is the first layer; the second layer is the clothing covering the figure.

Hip angle
The clothing is hiding the hips, so watch the hem when drawing a dress or skirt and match the hem to the hip angle.

The feet
Because the shoes are going to affect the height of the figure and change the angle of the foot, watch how the bottom of the foot is placed in your illustration.

▷ **TURN THE PAGE** For more on the clothed figure

Back view

In a back-view pose you are able to show the planes of the back. This is done by value contrast and curved clothing lines. The form of the body changes from the upper back plane, to the lower back plane, the pelvic box plane, and the lower pelvic box plane. If the upper back is lighter in value than the lower back, the form will show depth. The curves of the lines of clothing will follow the form of the shoulderline, the waistline, and the hipline.

Dress straps
Follow the shoulder relationship and form curves around the back of the upper torso.

Dress trim
Follows the form of the pelvic box and is higher on the left side of the figure.

Right leg
The leg farther away from you will be rendered a darker value to show depth.

Socks
Stripes follow the curve of the leg with the bend in the knees on both legs making a deep curve.

Back viewpoint
The spine is clearly showing on the nude, while the center back line in the clothed example is not obvious. Thinking about the location of the body parts will give you an edge in drawing any clothing, including this dress from a back view.

Feet and shoes
The left foot in this pose is on the ground in the nude and in a heel on the clothed figure. The foot is drawn differently in each example but the pose remains the same.

A pose from different angles

To understand the body means to be able to draw anything over it from any angle. As you begin to work with this concept you will understand how to draw horizontal and vertical curving lines as if they were illustrated over a solid figure. The benefits of understanding body lines and relationship angles is that you will be able to adjust the proportions of your figure and manipulate the pose as you choose.

Front pose
Here is an example of a three-quarter front view. The center front line is curving back because the torso is showing a spine back bend.

Side pose
Notice how the hips tip upward slightly. Watch the location of the hip angle and the center back line when it is all but hidden from view.

Back pose
Here is an example of the pose from a three-quarter back view. You can see the spine line of the center back clearly. The curved line follows the form of the body.

Curved lines on the bust apex
A key line on the body is the line drawn around the bust apex. In these poses, look for it to show you the way the body is shaped underneath.

Waist line
In all three examples the waist line is showing the model's right hip higher than her left hip. The most difficult view is the side view since it is not clear what is happening with the waist. You need to look at the hips to determine the waist angle on this side pose.

TECHNIQUE
19
The head guide

When you draw a head, work on illustrating the essence of the person. If you can capture the "feeling" of that particular person, you should end up with a much more creative and expressive illustration.

Beneath the skin

You need to look beneath the surface and see the individual character of each face you draw. Think, for example: if you wanted to describe a person's face, what two words would you use that would say something unique about it?

Technical considerations

As you begin to draw the face, look at how it is posed from your point of view and determine the eye level. If the model is seen straight on and there is no tipping of the head, you will see a slight curve to each feature as it is positioned around the form of the head. From the front, imaginary lines linking features will be curved; in effect resembling a smiling mouth. If you are viewing the head from above, the model and you have a high eye level, you will still see the features curving around the head at a deeper angle. If the model is higher than you and you have a low eye level, you will see the features curving in a frown-shaped curve around the head. The head is round, and all the facial features should be established around the curve of the basic form.

To establish the viewpoint, think of the face as part of the near-spherical head, and determine the spacing, the curve, and the proportions of each feature in relation to the entire head. See the illustrations on the opposite page to understand how this works.

Capturing the essence
This illustration is an example of drawing the "essence" of the model. Aim to draw more than a likeness; use your knowledge and intuition to express the person's mood and character.

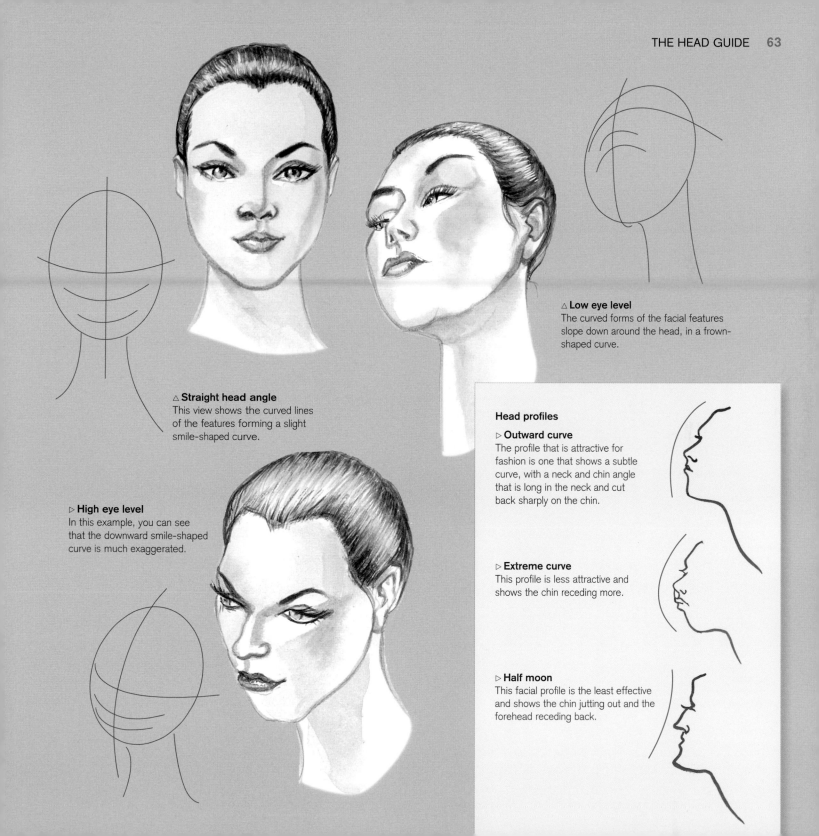

△ **Straight head angle**
This view shows the curved lines of the features forming a slight smile-shaped curve.

△ **Low eye level**
The curved forms of the facial features slope down around the head, in a frown-shaped curve.

▷ **High eye level**
In this example, you can see that the downward smile-shaped curve is much exaggerated.

Head profiles

▷ **Outward curve**
The profile that is attractive for fashion is one that shows a subtle curve, with a neck and chin angle that is long in the neck and cut back sharply on the chin.

▷ **Extreme curve**
This profile is less attractive and shows the chin receding more.

▷ **Half moon**
This facial profile is the least effective and shows the chin jutting out and the forehead receding back.

Male and female faces

The features of both sexes are spaced in the same way, and the construction of all parts of the face looks similar. The line of the jaw is often more prominent and square-shaped in a male face. The eyebrows of a male figure are also usually thicker. The female face is rounder, while the male face is more angular. These are guidelines and are not firm rules. Every face is unique, so look at different examples and discover the many possible unconventional qualities. The concept known as *jolie laide* (French for pretty/ugly) is based on seeing the beauty in a face that is unconventional or not considered pretty but still has its own distinctive harmony or charm.

Neck length
One face has a short neck and the other a longer neck. The fashion model has a longer neck and this is to show more elegance and graceful curves of the head and neck angle.

Same on both male and female head
• Eye line
• Nose placement
• Mouth placement

Female head
• Rounder forms on all contours
• Thinner eyebrows
• Thinner neck that curves inward
• Round chin

Male head
• Sharper angles on all contours
• Thicker eyebrows
• Straighter neck
• Square chin

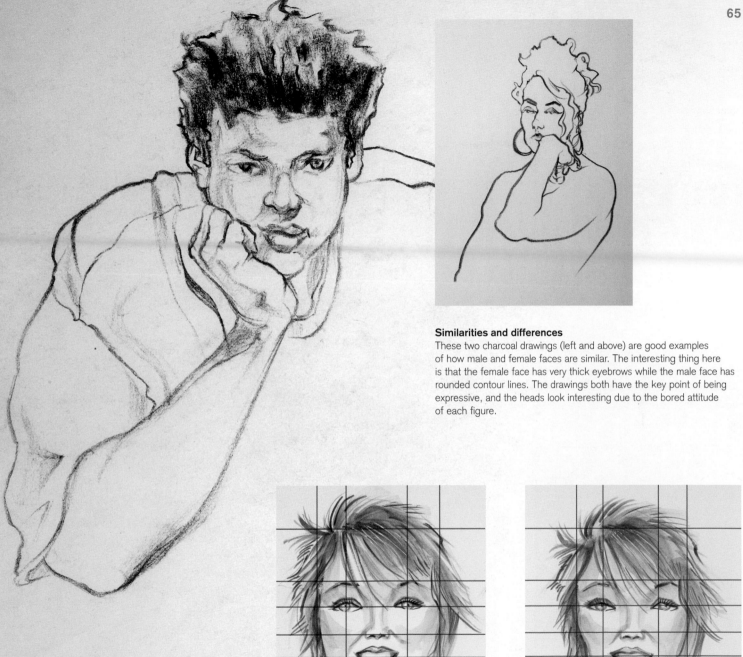

Similarities and differences

These two charcoal drawings (left and above) are good examples of how male and female faces are similar. The interesting thing here is that the female face has very thick eyebrows while the male face has rounded contour lines. The drawings both have the key point of being expressive, and the heads look interesting due to the bored attitude of each figure.

Recognition through shape

Facial proportions and the overall shape of the face are what cause us to recognize a person, more than the details of the individual features. This illustration shows a face drawn with identical features but two face shapes. The outer face shape is the determining factor for recognition and likeness.

20 Skin

There is a wide variety of possible skin tones and depicting them can be one of the most rewarding parts of drawing the head and face. Skin is luminous and is capable of showing complex and radiant color. This luminous quality is consistent in every face, regardless of skin tone and, if captured successfully, can light up your fashion illustration.

Skin tones

Observe and draw the skin tone with light and dark values and seek to see the accent colors that have nothing to do with realistic color. Many great fashion illustrations owe their expressive mood to not copying the exact skin tones in a photographic way.

1 Draw the background color and value all over the face, leaving white paper only in the whites of the eyes.

Planes of the face

When showing the planes of the face, the idea is to find a way to show two main values: one is the light and one is the shadow. To see and depict these shapes, simplify the planes: for example, the eye sockets are dark, along with one side of the nose; the neck is dark and the color can be depicted in two or more values.

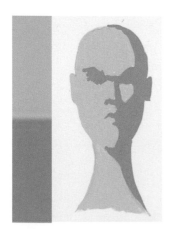

△ **Curved**
The illustration shows curved shapes and light skin tones, with light and shadow effects.

△ **Sharp**
The illustration shows angular shapes and a dark skin tone, with light and shadow effects.

2 Using a second (and darker) color and value for the sides of the face and the neck, create shadow shapes that illustrate planes of the face. The second dark value can depict lips, hair, and eye sockets.

3 Add more details including the outlines around the face, the facial hair dots and texture details, and use white paint to highlight the lips, nose, and top accent planes of the face.

Non-realistic color

The use of non-realistic color can be a fun way to make a fantastic drawing. Since the character of a face is established in the drawing, you can create fantasy color for parts of the face. The skin tones, the hair, and all other aspects of the drawing can be a surprise for the viewer through use of color that shows expression and isn't photographic in its representation.

Unconventional
This illustration depicts a green face with gold and orange accents. The hair is depicted in brown, and there is a feeling for character in part due to the unconventional color choices. The lighting effect clearly shows the planes of the face.

TECHNIQUE

21

Facial features

The individual features that make up a face and the way you position them can be determined according to certain rules. Once you have understood these rules, play around with them to create an infinite variety of faces.

Constructing the face and features

Look at the space between the eyes, nose, and mouth. Check the distance between the mouth and the chin. It is essential to study proportions as you depict a face. There is more distance between the eyes and nose than there is between the nose and mouth. It is often helpful to draw a center front line on the face to line up the features against.

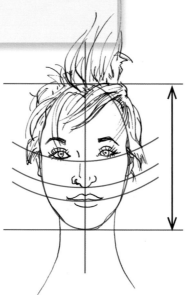

1 Construct the basic outline of the face.

2 Create the drawing in pencil and then apply color to the main planes. These include the eye sockets, the cheekbones, and the neck. In this example, the face is created with watercolor by using the "wet-in-wet" technique.

3 Create a second layer, where the face is completed with the makeup. This example is illustrated in watercolor and the hair is drawn in dry-brush watercolor layers.

Eyes

The eyes are where the viewer tends to look first, when seeing a person. Draw your illustrations with eyes that are bright and shiny—the eye is a wet surface and needs to be glossy. Draw a highlight after rendering the color by using a white gel pen or a drop of opaque gouache paint on the iris.

The iris is an elliptical shape and the lids overlap this to form two white triangles—the "whites" of the eyes. If you look at these shapes and see which one is larger you can get a good feeling for the design of the eye. Look at the axis between the inner and outer eye corner from a front view to determine the angle of each face you draw.

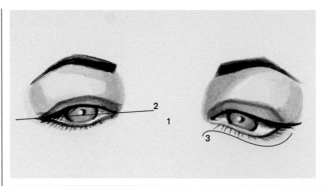

1. Space between
Leave more than one eye width between eyes for a more dreamy, "fashion" expression.

2. Axis direction
From a front view, the inner and outer corners will show you how to see the axis direction of the eye. In this example, the outer corner is lower than the inner corner.

3. Curved lines
Eyes include s-shaped curves. See how the curve is compound and will alternate direction in one contour line area.

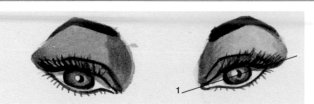

1. Axis direction
The inner corner in this example shows a lower angle than the outer corner.

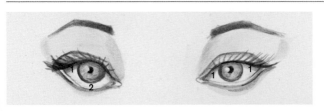

1. Cast shadow
Show a shadow shape below the upper eyelid to depict depth.

2. Fashion eye
This example shows a "dreamy" eye—this effect is achieved by showing more white space beneath the iris shape.

1. Side view
This example demonstrates how the lid of the eye shows width or thickness in the lower eyelid, and how the iris is an elliptical shape.

2. Three-quarter side view
The nose overlaps the eye in this view, and there is a full eye-width between the eyes to allow for the appearance of the bridge of the nose.

1. Eye color
The shiny, reflective quality of an eye shows shades that vary within each eye color. Brown eyes can be gold and brown. Green eyes can be green, gold, and blue/green. The outer corner of each eye is darker than the inner eye in the iris area.

2. Watercolor washes
Use "wet-in-wet" watercolor wash to depict the eyes. Allow the paint to run and bleed into the water. Complete the look with pencil lines over the shapes of color.

3. White space
Look for the shapes and draw these carefully. You will usually see triangle-shaped white spaces on the eyes.

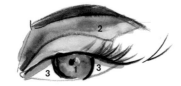

Ears

Ears are spiral-shaped and tilt back on the head at a diagonal directional angle from a side view. Work on the curves and how they overlap from all views. The back view is particularly fun to draw since it shows the elegant shape of the outer ear curving in front of the back of the ear.

Nose

Check your viewpoint and eye level to determine the shape and contours of the nose. The nose is a complicated shape with a center plane and two side planes. There is a curved ball shape at the tip of the nose and the nostrils complete the picture. To depict the side view, show the tip of the nose overlapping the nostril behind. From a low eye level, draw the nostrils with more angularity. Avoid drawing simple round dots for nostrils.

Mouth

Check the center front line and draw all the parts of the lips with overlapping forms. The mouth has an upper lip center curve—or dip—at the top, and the lips will stretch in a smile causing them to have less fullness than a non-smiling mouth. Observe your view and find the center front before drawing the upper and lower sections.

Facial characterization
Notice that the figure's face in a full figure illustration is only a focus when a mood or expression needs to be conveyed. The main emphasis on the face shows us what is going on in the mind of the model. Drawing this with skill is an essential ingredient when creating good illustrations of the whole body. Contrary to what may be a popular stylization, leaving the face as a blank space on a full figure drawing is a mistake that will cost the viewer the chance to see more depth in your illustration.

Hairline
The hairline is a heart-shaped curve, and hair growth occurs on this line. The line needs to be clearly stated but is not really a continuous line; it is a non-enclosed line made of small strokes that stem from it, as shown in this illustration.

Hairline
The hairline follows a heart-shaped form on the top.

Center front line
Find the center front line, and draw the tip of the nose and the center dip on the upper lip aligned with this vertical line.

Back view ear
The ear seen from the back is an overlapping width followed by the curves of the ear back.

Ear tilted back
Tip the ear back from a side view so there is a slight diagonal line.

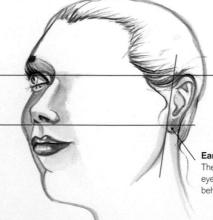

Ear location
The ears are located between the eyes and the nose on a vertical line, behind the jawline.

DRAWING THE HEAD AND FACE—CHECKLIST:

• Look beyond the "technical considerations"—try to capture the essence of the person's face.

• Decide the eye level from which you are viewing the face. This will determine the positioning of the features around the head.

• There are broad differences between male and female faces. But there are no hard and fast rules; some male faces will show "female" characteristics, and vice versa.

• The overall shape of the face is the determining factor in recognition, rather than the individual features.

• When depicting the planes of the face, simplify the skin tones into a range of two or three values.

TECHNIQUE

22 Hairstyles

The way to approach hair is to draw the shape of the hairstyle and then observe the highlighted areas within this shape. Hair is glossy and reflective. There is always a highlight running through the strands of hair. You should find the place where this occurs on the crown of the head.

△ **Hair with unrealistic color**
This drawing was created on a sheet of black paper using dry pastel. The strands of hair are not simply depicting a hair color but are creating a mood and expression of anger. The red, blue, and yellow strands are helping to depict this mood.

Hair color

Make a study of the possible colors of hair. Hair can be dark or light, so look for the basic hair color and work on seeing it as lighter and darker values within this main color. There can be reflective colors in hair, as well as unrealistic colors for a fashion drawing. Try drawing blue hair, for example, for a fun expression.

▷ **Curly hair**
The individual strands can be drawn as shapes, and the highlight is on the crown of the head.

▷ **Highlight shape**
Leave the white of the paper showing for highlights to show volume in the hair.

▷ **Short hair**
This style is composed of many different overlapping strands. Begin with the top and work downward on the drawing of each strand as you tuck one piece of hair behind another.

▷ **Straight hair**
This example shows the strands separating at the ends. Use a heavy pressure on the medium and then lighten your touch as you end the mark for each strand.

▷ **Clipped-up hairstyle**
The knot on top of the head is the predominant hair shape here. Outlining the edges of this shape and then filling in the individual strands will create the look of each part of this style.

▷ **Hair in motion**
When a model walks, her hair will swing out in a fluid shape. Capture this motion by drawing the individual strands as separate pieces at the end of the main shape.

◁ **Bright red hair**
This figure has a base hair color of red. The vibrant color depicted is slightly brighter to enhance the mood of the illustration and create more sizzle and sexuality. The color is also brighter to accentuate the black dress the model is wearing.

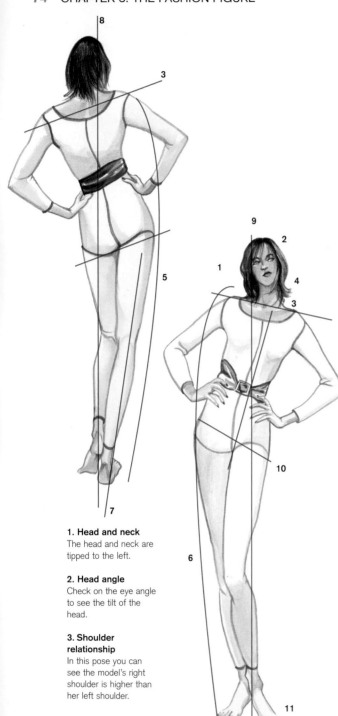

Key angles and lines

TECHNIQUE 23

The trick to drawing a good croquis figure lies in finding the body's main directional angles and lines. These include the head angle, the neck angle, the shoulder relationship angle, the center front or back line, the balance line and locating the leg with the most weight; as well as finding the directional angle of the legs, the hip angle, and the relationship of the feet. Look for the leading edge of the figure where you see the most "thrust." This usually comes from the hip.

The sum of the parts

To ensure successful figure drawing, take a look at the position of the parts. Figure out where you can exaggerate a relationship and still have a well-drawn figure. Since all the parts move and hinge together, changing the pose of one area will affect all the others. For example, a slight movement in the shoulders to show one higher than another will cause the hips to shift in an opposing movement. Understanding these interrelated movements comes from careful study of the figure. When you can draw the body well, you can manipulate the pose angles to increase expression.

1. Head and neck
The head and neck are tipped to the left.

2. Head angle
Check on the eye angle to see the tilt of the head.

3. Shoulder relationship
In this pose you can see the model's right shoulder is higher than her left shoulder.

4. Neck angle
When the head moves, the neck stretches with it and changes direction. Here, the model's left eye is higher than her right, causing her neck to stretch to the left.

5. Balance line
This is the key to manipulating the figure. The balance line is one that shows where the sides of the figure line up as the relationship angles are formed.

6. Leading edge
This is the line of the figure that has the most action. In this example, the model is thrusting her hip to the left.

7. Supporting leg directional angle
The supporting leg is the one with the most weight. Watch the directional diagonal it is showing, as the hip is thrust out. The more hip thrust you have, the greater the diagonal directional angle you will see on the supporting leg.

8. Center back line
You can see a diagonal directional angle on this pose in the center back line.

9. Center front line
This pose shows the center front line as a diagonal line.

10. Hip relationship
The model's right hip is higher than her left hip.

11. Feet placement and relationship
The feet will create the support for the pose, so drawing them at the correct angle is an essential part of depicting the pose.

Male and female figures

When creating poses for a female figure, exaggerate the hip thrust. Attitude is conveyed through the facial expression and body angles. You can see in the examples on page 74 that the figure of the female model is created with a more "pushed" leading edge than the male figure. The male model (right) is tipping his chin up and the female model is tipping her chin down a little.

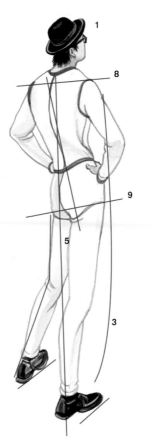

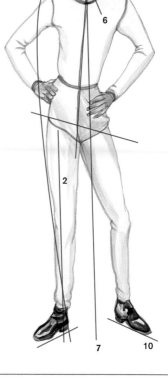

1. Head angle
The chin is tipped up.

2. Balance line and supporting leg directional angle
The supporting leg is almost straight, while the opposite leg is bent.

3. Leading edge
The right hip is thrust out—establish this first.

4. Head and neck
The chin is tipped up and the neck is stretched forward.

5. Center back line
There is an s-shaped curve in the back.

6. Neck angle
The model stretches his neck to the right.

7. Center front line
The center front line is slightly diagonal.

8. Shoulder angle
The model's right shoulder is a little higher than his left.

9. Hip relationship
The model's right hip is higher than his left hip.

10. Feet angle relationship
Each foot is pointing in a different diagonal direction.

Eye level and the figure

When you begin to understand how to draw the body angles, you can then pay attention to the curving of all the angles around a basic pose. If clothing on the body is at a straight angle, it is exactly at eye level. The curves of the clothing above the eye level are often curved downward at the corners. Clothing that is below eye level is often curved up at the corners. Clothing will curve around all forms in S-shaped curves.

Three-quarter front view
Here you can see a little of the side plane of the figure and more of the front plane.

1. Above eye level
You can see the form of the bracelet as an example of a frown-shaped curve.

2. Eye level
This pose is a straight eye level pose. The clothing is shown to curve around the form of the figure.

3. Eye level
This is where clothing lines appear fairly straight.

4. Neckline
The s-shaped curve is a result of the shoulder relationship and the fact that the model's left shoulder is higher than her right one.

5. Below eye level
You can see a smile-shaped curve on the below eye level forms. The shirt has a hemline that illustrates this concept.

6. Pants hemline
Another s-shaped curve line.

⟶ **TURN THE PAGE** For viewpoint and developing poses

TECHNIQUE 24
Viewpoint

Take a look at a dress form and observe it from all three views (straight, above, and below). Look at the form from a straight view and the waistline appears to be a straight angle. You can look from a high eye level (looking down at the subject) and see the waist curve upward on the corners with the "smile" curve. The final option is to view the form from below and see how the waistline curves down in the "frown" curve.

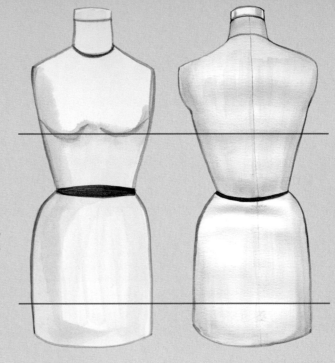

Front or back view
These two illustrations depict a front and a back view at eye level. Note the way the curves are formed on the waist, the neckline, and on the lower torso.

△ **Front view**   △ **Back view**

Dress form from the front
The three front views of the dress form clearly show the curves that occur on the figure. Although these forms have straight shoulder and hip relationships, they allow you to see the principle of the construction lines around the body and how the viewer's eye level affects the way they are formed.

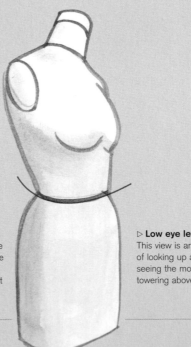
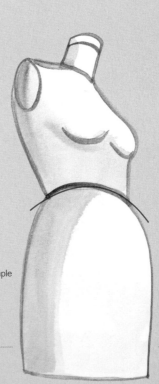

▷ **High eye level**
This view is one where you look down on the pose or subject matter.

▷ **Straight eye level**
This view is one where you look straight at the model and your eyes are at the same height as the model's eyes.

▷ **Low eye level**
This view is an example of looking up and seeing the model towering above you.

Developing poses

TECHNIQUE 25

There are many ways to go about developing poses for fashion illustration. The use of reference material is an important part of pose development. You can use magazine photos of models or take your own reference photos. Alter the basic pose and reproportion the figure to your desired length. You can also develop the pose to enhance the expression by exaggerating the angles of the body and by changing the position of a hand or foot.

Adjusting the pose

You often only have to make minor adjustments to the placement of the body parts to convey a different attitude in an illustration. This process demonstrates a way to exaggerate both proportions and pose elements to portray a garment detail or the mood of a collection through the model's pose.

The croquis figure needs to reflect a collection's spirit. You can achieve this by manipulating the model's pose. For instance, you could use one head angle and a different body as necessary for a particular garment to be shown to advantage. The head, arms, and the legs are the main areas to refine. However, the torso also conveys expressive information so watch how you draw the curve of the spine when you want to exaggerate a pose.

1. Head angle
In this pose you can see the model tipping her chin down, and her expression is one of relaxed confidence with a slight touch of whimsy.

2. The torso
This figure has a straighter spine and the body seems to be less flirty and more refined in posture and attitude.

3. The arms
In this view the arms are covering the torso. This might cause problems when the figure is clothed because they may obscure critical garment details.

4. The legs
This pose is a good example of showing the legs overlapped and could work well for many garments, including dresses or skirts.

5. The legs
The legs in this pose are not overlapped. Garments that might benefit from the clarity of this view would include pants.

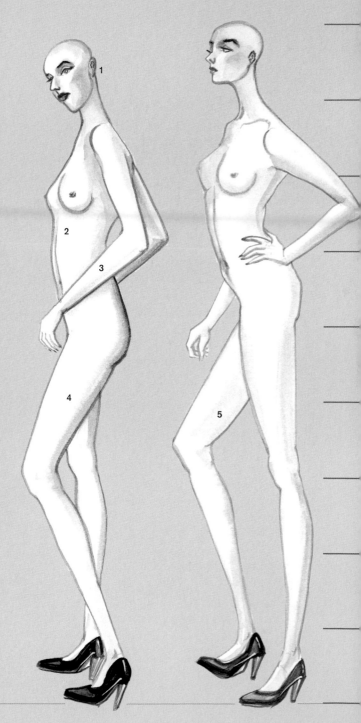

TECHNIQUE 26 Refining a pose

It is a good idea to save magazine photographs of models as reference that shows hands, arms, and legs in a wide variety of poses. This type of reference source is known as a "scrap file." When you work on croquis figures, you can use this reference material and refine it using tracing paper overlays. This process is known as "refining the pose," and the idea is to improve on the original pose using the under-layers as a guide. It allows you to create a well-drawn figure to suit your needs; as opposed to simply tracing a figure and changing nothing. Refining a pose is a fun way to get a wide variety of poses and also save time.

1 Find a photo of a figure wearing underwear. Draw this pose.

2 Place tracing paper over the first drawing, and draw a second version. Refine the parts you wish to change. In this example, the neck was elongated, the arms were depicted as slightly longer and narrower, the legs were reduced in width, and the torso was elongated.

3 Find other photos of figures with the same shoulder and hip relationships, but different arm arrangements, a different head angle, and different leg angles. Place tracing paper over the drawing from Step 2 and redraw the main body, while creating a new head, arms, and legs.

Using overlays

Developing poses is an art that takes time to master. The pose of the male figure in the final illustration (opposite) is the end product of five drawings created sequentially on tracing paper overlays, and three different pieces of photo reference.

The method

One way to work is to draw a rough of the pose on a piece of tracing paper that is then placed over a proportion guide (see page 48). After deciding on the measurements of this guide—anything between eight and ten heads in length—draw the original rough sketch on the first piece of tracing paper. Then, when creating a second tracing paper layer, redraw the pose to get better proportions, and fine-tune the hands, feet, and face. Develop the detailed parts on layer two or three, after you get the main pose lines together. The number of layers will vary. Finally, the illustration is complete when the last layer is satisfactory and you feel ready to use it as a basis for the finished piece. Use a lightbox to transfer the final drawing to a piece of paper. The pose can later be reused, flopped or altered in a minor way each time you use it.

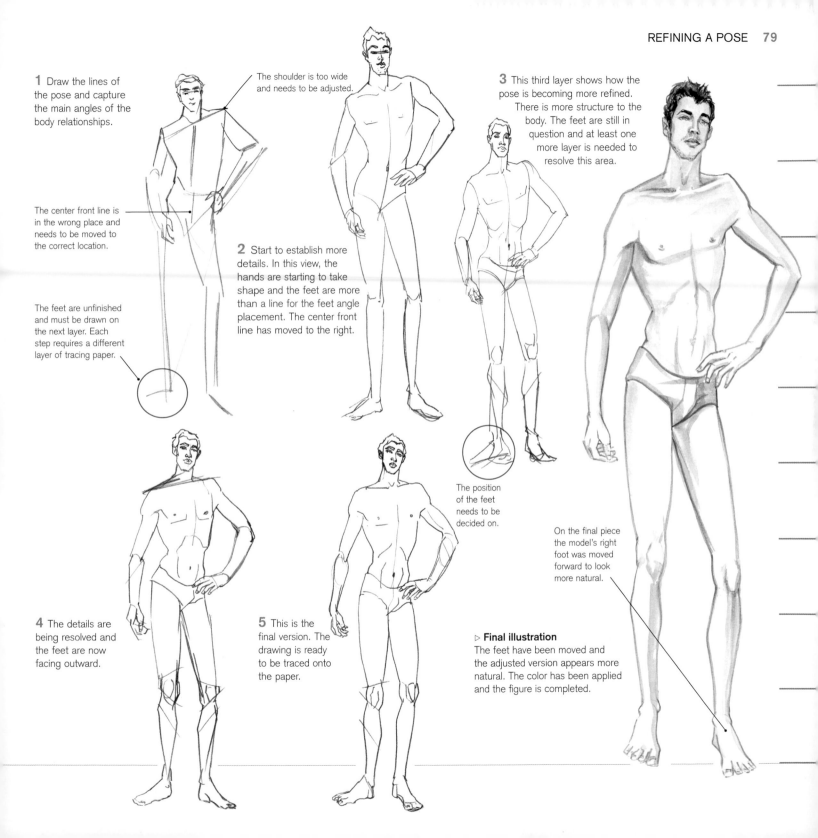

1 Draw the lines of the pose and capture the main angles of the body relationships.

The shoulder is too wide and needs to be adjusted.

The center front line is in the wrong place and needs to be moved to the correct location.

The feet are unfinished and must be drawn on the next layer. Each step requires a different layer of tracing paper.

2 Start to establish more details. In this view, the hands are starting to take shape and the feet are more than a line for the feet angle placement. The center front line has moved to the right.

3 This third layer shows how the pose is becoming more refined. There is more structure to the body. The feet are still in question and at least one more layer is needed to resolve this area.

The position of the feet needs to be decided on.

On the final piece the model's right foot was moved forward to look more natural.

4 The details are being resolved and the feet are now facing outward.

5 This is the final version. The drawing is ready to be traced onto the paper.

▷ **Final illustration**
The feet have been moved and the adjusted version appears more natural. The color has been applied and the figure is completed.

To look with a critical eye at the inside of the figure and see how important it is in drawing the clothed figure is the focus of this chapter. Drawing using guidelines is a way to ensure uniformity of the proportions. Knowledge of drawing the key lines over a body as you develop the croquis figure is essential in being able to depict difficult, body-hiding clothing. You will learn to look for the center front and back lines as well as the waist to show better form. Mapping an imagined garment will become easier with the knowledge of the garment construction lines.

4

Techniques

Illustration basics

TECHNIQUE 27

When illustrating fashion for a finished portfolio piece, the designer or illustrator must consider many aspects of the job. Dividing the process into a series of steps is one way to simplify the technique of illustrating a portfolio piece.

RENDERING DECISIONS

The main choices involved in creating a finished piece are deciding what media to use, determining the technique, and finally mapping the garment to be illustrated onto a prepared figure.

The media is often mixed, with layers of wet or dry media. You may choose to fully color and render the entire figure in a "realistic" manner. Or you may color only the shadow shapes and leave white paper with no paint on it to depict form and "spare-out" white. Or you can use a rendering approach where part of the figure is rendered and part is drawn. The choice will be based on your own preferences as well as how much time is available.

THE POSE

Start with a pose and then resolve the forms of the figure. Get the proportions, the viewpoint, and the basics established. Do you want to use a front, a side, or a back pose in your final illustration? What is the eye level of the viewpoint? Do you need a low eye level for more dramatic expression? Will a side pose best show aspects of the garment? Ask yourself these questions before starting the illustration.

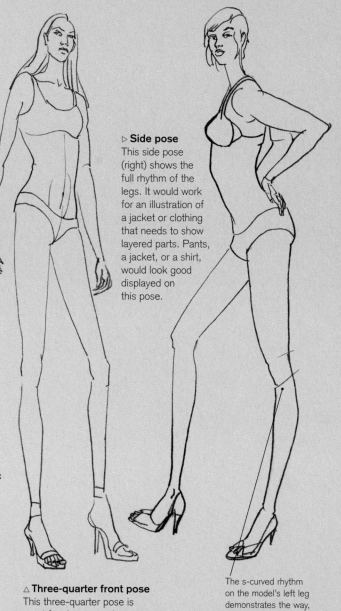

▷ **Side pose**
This side pose (right) shows the full rhythm of the legs. It would work for an illustration of a jacket or clothing that needs to show layered parts. Pants, a jacket, or a shirt, would look good displayed on this pose.

△ **Three-quarter front pose**
This three-quarter pose is great for showing a dramatic view of a long dress. It is a low eye level pose seen from below.

The s-curved rhythm on the model's left leg demonstrates the way, in the body, one form curves against another.

FLOPPING THE POSE

When you have developed a pose, it is easy to take this pose and "flop" the figure to face the opposite direction. This is one way in which you can get more range out of a pose you have developed.

Clothed side pose figure
Here, the side pose figure has had clothing mapped onto it (see page 84) but has not been flopped.

Flopped illustration
The same pose was flopped and transferred to a piece of paper, then clothing was mapped onto it and rendered in color. In this example, the hairstyle has been changed and a basket accessory was added to the figure. An arm was developed to grasp the handle of the basket.

GARMENT CONSTRUCTION LINES

There are a few lines that are especially helpful when you are drawing clothing over a refined croquis figure. These lines include the center front line, the center back line, the bust apex, the waistline, the armholes, the princess seams, and the panty lines. If you draw these lines on top of the refined drawing of the body, you can follow them when you work on mapping a garment over the figure. Mapping is a particular way of designing the structured lines of clothing on top of a three-dimensional surface.

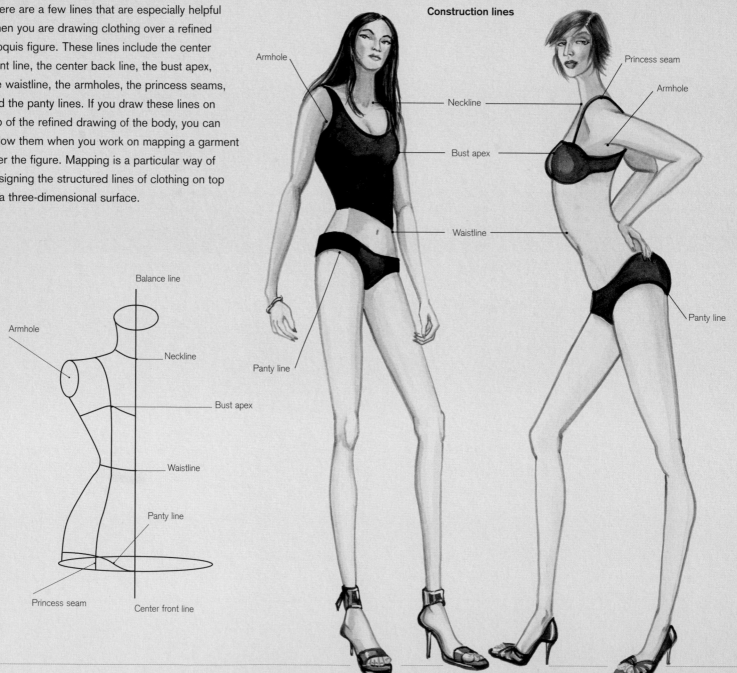

Balance line

Armhole

Neckline

Bust apex

Waistline

Panty line

Princess seam

Center front line

Construction lines

Armhole

Neckline

Bust apex

Waistline

Panty line

Princess seam

Armhole

Waistline

Panty line

TECHNIQUE
28 Forms and garment types

The illustration of all clothing depends on the shape and form of the garments to be depicted. For example, if you are drawing pants and a T-shirt, there are different rules to work with than if you are drawing a long gown.

The main considerations when drawing garments include the location and careful placement of seam lines, the understanding of eye level when drawing the clothes on a figure, and the illustration of folds. The first step is to learn about the guidelines for drawing the main garment types.

FLATS AND CLOTHING DETAILS

In a flat version of an illustration, an article of clothing appears to show an obvious shape and all the construction lines are clearly stated. You will see that drawing the same item over a figure, showing form and dimension, is more of a challenge. The first thing to consider is the shape of the garment. All clothing must appear to flow and have volume when depicted on a figure. This is achieved through careful mapping of the flat illustration.

Flat jacket

Croquis figure

Flat skirt

1 The shape and construction lines of the flat garments are established and the croquis figure is drawn.

2 The flat garments are mapped onto the croquis figure.

3 The mapped clothing is then rendered on the pose.

➤ TURN THE PAGE For more forms and garment types

SKIRTS

Garment forms include variations of skirts. Skirts have folds that form from the hip to the knee. Hemlines follow hip angles and the seam lines curve around the body in such a way that the figure is depicted under the clothes.

TOPS

The depiction of shirts, jackets, and all other clothing items that will be illustrated on the upper torso is based on finding the center front line of the body. After the pose is depicted, the clothing is drawn to show the details, which includes folds, seam lines, and neckline shapes.

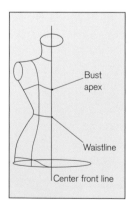

Bust apex

Waistline

Center front line

The curves of each armhole show the main angle of each pose.

Folds that form around the connection point of the end of the pelvic box and the beginning of the leg.

Princess seams

◁ △ **Garment forms**
These figures are wearing a variety of clothing types, and in each case the forms of the garments are clearly stated.

▷ **Back view**
The white dress depicted in this example shows how the center back line is an important consideration when drawing the back straps that cross exactly at the spine. The double skirt shows folds that cascade down in triangular shapes.

▽ **Low eye level view**
This figure is seen from a low eye level and the shorter skirt's hemline follows the angle of the hips. You can see the more elaborate neckline and the ruffled collar as a form that is clearly depicted with a center front placement that matches the pose. The low eye level results in a waistline that is curved in a frown-shaped angle.

∧ **Bent leg**
This example of pants and T-shirt combined with a heavy sweater shows how you must consider the knee when drawing the bend in the leg. The pants form folds that curve outward on the side of the knee. The straight leg shows the side seam, and this adds rhythm to the pose.

▭▷ **TURN THE PAGE** For more forms and garment types

CENTER FRONT LINE

It is important to locate the center front line of the figure when drawing an illustration. If the pose is a simple front view, the clothing mapped onto it will have almost the same amount of space on each side.

When the pose is a view from the side, or a three-quarter front view, the placement of the center front line will mean that the clothing shows more on one side than on the other. This affects both the bodice and the pants shapes. You will notice that the illustration on page 85 has a center front line on a croquis figure. Now you can see how this becomes a great tool when you are drawing clothing forms.

Note the placement of the neckline

Note the placement of the neckline

See how the pants are almost even on each side of the center front line.

This illustration shows a figure with a center front line marked by the blouse's button placement and the collar at the base of the neck. The three-quarter front view clearly shows the way the blouse has been drawn with a wider left bodice and narrow right side.

The pants form uneven shapes on this pose. The right side is smaller than the left side.

Bust apex

Waistline

Center front line

Symmetrical front view pose
Here is an easy-to-find center front line. The pose is a front view with the v-shaped bodice neckline located on the center front line. Both the right and left sides of this bodice are mapped onto the pose easily, with each side being similar in shape.

Three-quarter side view pose
This pose shows the center front line creating the v-shaped bodice more to the model's right. You can see the jacket is formed with a wider left side and a narrower right side, due to the pose.

CENTER BACK LINE

The center back line of the body can assist you in drawing many clothing forms—it will help you establish the main thrust of the pose from a back view. When illustrating garment forms from the back, the spine will appear in a gown with a low cut back.

Other clothing forms, including jackets and shirts, often don't show the spine, which is the figure's key anatomical structure point from behind. So the use of a center back line is an abstract concept to help you map the garments' directional forms and folds as well as the patterns of the clothes from a back view.

Curved spine

Here the figure is curving her spine in a back bend. With the center back as a guide to locating the shirt, skirt, and the hip angle, you can see how a strong understanding of this tool helps to show curves on the waist, the bottom of the shirt, and the hemline.

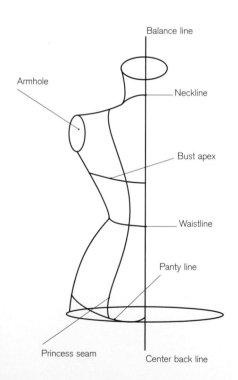

Balance line

Armhole

Neckline

Bust apex

Waistline

Panty line

Princess seam

Center back line

Center back detail

This illustration shows an inset piece of fabric that is placed on the center back line position. You can use such a detail to show the pose angle and place the details perfectly in line with the body.

Back view

The complex quilted pattern is illustrated by showing the figures curving around the back, and the center back line is useful in helping keep track of where the design is located.

▭▷ **TURN THE PAGE** For more forms and garment types

Armhole
There is only one armhole to draw on this dress. It curves around the forms of the torso and should be large enough to show the full shoulder structure.

GUIDELINES

The use of guidelines is essential when illustrating the complicated lines of the fold structure on a garment. You will find it helpful to draw the curve of the bust line, the waistline, the hemline, and the center front and back lines. The vertical fold lines, when dropped from the waist, can show you the curve of the pelvic box. The hem may be illustrated through knowledge of the hip angles and will depend on the figure's pose. The draped structure of a garment can be planned around these key lines of the figure.

Neckline
This dress has an off-the-shoulder construction, causing the curve to follow the lines of the figure, and the key construction line of the neckline is not a typical curve. The solution to the drawing of this curve is to form it around the figure in a curve that shows volume.

Back waistline
From this view, the waistline is curved upward.

Front waistline
This example shows a downward curve and is higher on the model's left side.

Three-quarter front pose
You can see how the forms of the bodice folds curve around the shape of the breasts and also clearly form a diagonal directional angle crossing the center front line.

Back view
In this example, the center back line is helpful in forming the overlapping curve of the bodice. Notice that the underneath part of the left side of the bodice is curving exactly to the center back point. There is a zipper on the dress at this point that is hidden from view.

Front hemline
The hem curves downward and is higher on the model's left side since the figure's left hip is higher than her right hip.

Back hemline
The hem curves upward from the back view. The model is posing with a strong back bend and the center back placement is essential in showing how to draw the folds on the skirt of the dress.

▷ Side of the body
The folds are straighter on the side, while to the left and right of the side line you can see the directional angles change and curve around the pelvic box structure.

▷ Back bend pose
This is a clear view of the pose showing the model's spine tilted at a strong angle. The pelvic box is clearly pushed backward while the upper torso is tilted backward.

Center back line
This back pose is showing the hip angle more clearly. You can see the way the model's left hip is higher than her right, and the way this affects the waistline, hemline, and neckline.

Hemline
The hem will curve with the hip angle, and an understanding of the pelvic box will help you to create a successful curve.

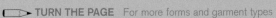
TURN THE PAGE   For more forms and garment types

SEWING LINES

The guidelines that tell you where sewing lines exist on many garments are good ones to draw. The neckline is a key guideline and so is the armhole. Looking at the armhole, you can observe how the sleeve is set into the garment and how large the armhole area is.

Princess seams show the construction of garment parts and are also key guidelines. Look at a wide variety of garment forms and you will see that to illustrate them well, the seam lines and garment construction lines are an essential part of drawing convincing clothing over a body.

▽ **Neckline**
This dress features a low neckline and the shape of it is curving downward to show the center front of the figure. The neckline acts as a guideline that shows you the placement of the collar and its width. The sleeves are set into this dress to show the shoulder width and form and the armholes are curved backward toward the tops of the shoulders.

Princess seams
This model is wearing a blouse that is shaped around the princess seams—the panels that make up the blouse are cut wider at the bottom than the top. The neckline is square and the armholes are formed by the tie at the side seam of the garment, illustrating the importance of seam and garment construction guidelines.

Realism
The dress features a square neckline and princess seams. These details are helpful in establishing the construction of this garment and they also add to the feeling of realism.

Form and volume
This suit shows the depiction of princess seams on a jacket and dress. The collar follows the neckline and it shows a curved form with fabric width. The armholes are drawn as raglan sleeves. The illustration shows clothing that fits well and is full of form and volume. The buttons on the jacket front define the center front line of this illustration. This example illustrates many of the garment construction lines.

TURN THE PAGE For mapping

TECHNIQUE 29 Mapping

The way to envision how a garment will look on a figure is to use a concept known as "mapping." Mapping involves taking imaginary lines of clothing and plotting them onto a figure's form through the use of a grid. The grid is placed over the body and provides a way to chart clothing lines, folds, and details of garments over a figure.

Find a point on the grid that matches where the collar point is located and create a dot on that point. Then find another point for the placement of the next segment of collar and draw a line between the points.

Anatomy and the fashion figure
The bony structure of the body is underneath all of the skin, muscles, and clothing forms.

When placing a grid over the body, the curving lines form contours around, across, and over the figure. If the grid were flat, you would see square-shaped forms. As the grid is stretched over a figure, the squares become lines that curve around the figure and form a map for placing clothing lines, folds, and design details over it.

Mapping and grid lines
The beauty of mapping is that you don't need to have a garment to illustrate. Garments that exist only in your mind can be mapped on top of a figure, and you will see the vision that was previously only in your head translated onto paper. Alternately, you can draw a flat illustration of the garment you wish to map and use it as a reference when mapping it onto a posed body.

Points on the croquis figure
The jacket is drawn by finding a point on the flat illustration and then where it would be located on the three-dimensional figure, and continuing this process until many of the points are located. Finally, the points are lined up with a contour line and the jacket emerges on the paper. This process is best done in overlays using trace.

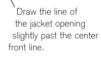

Draw the line of the jacket opening slightly past the center front line.

A flat grid pattern

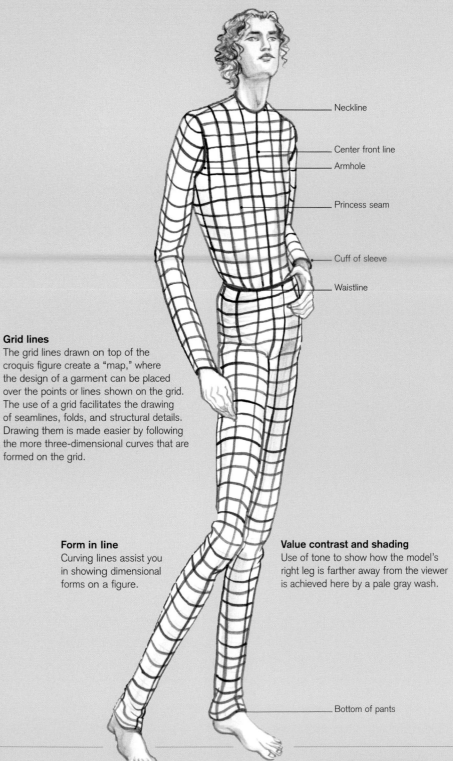

Neckline

Center front line

Armhole

Princess seam

Cuff of sleeve

Waistline

Grid lines
The grid lines drawn on top of the
croquis figure create a "map," where
the design of a garment can be placed
over the points or lines shown on the grid.
The use of a grid facilitates the drawing
of seamlines, folds, and structural details.
Drawing them is made easier by following
the more three-dimensional curves that are
formed on the grid.

Form in line
Curving lines assist you
in showing dimensional
forms on a figure.

Value contrast and shading
Use of tone to show how the model's
right leg is farther away from the viewer
is achieved here by a pale gray wash.

Bottom of pants

▷ **TURN THE PAGE** For more mapping

MAPPING CASE STUDY

Take a look at this case study in developing a pose, mapping a garment over the pose, and using all the garment construction lines to help you in the process. You can develop each illustration in stages, taking these steps in the production of your croquis figures.

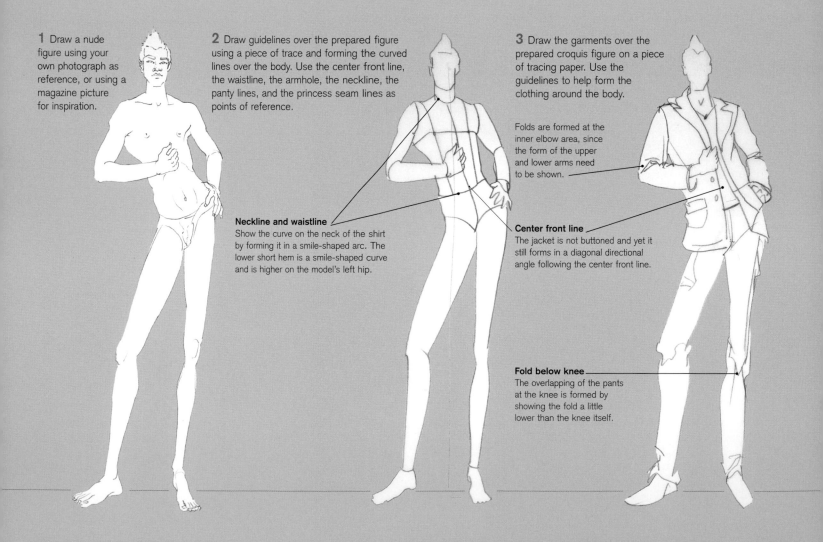

1 Draw a nude figure using your own photograph as reference, or using a magazine picture for inspiration.

2 Draw guidelines over the prepared figure using a piece of trace and forming the curved lines over the body. Use the center front line, the waistline, the armhole, the neckline, the panty lines, and the princess seam lines as points of reference.

Neckline and waistline
Show the curve on the neck of the shirt by forming it in a smile-shaped arc. The lower short hem is a smile-shaped curve and is higher on the model's left hip.

3 Draw the garments over the prepared croquis figure on a piece of tracing paper. Use the guidelines to help form the clothing around the body.

Folds are formed at the inner elbow area, since the form of the upper and lower arms need to be shown.

Center front line
The jacket is not buttoned and yet it still forms in a diagonal directional angle following the center front line.

Fold below knee
The overlapping of the pants at the knee is formed by showing the fold a little lower than the knee itself.

4 Draw the under layer of color in your chosen media. Here, some watercolor washes were applied to the figure in two values.

5 Complete the figure using more surface texture and drawing more details.

▶ **TURN THE PAGE** For folds and draping

TECHNIQUE
Folds and draping

Folds are important to fashion illustration because they show the structure of the garments being depicted. Folds that are draped into the clothes and are sewn in place include tucked, pleated, shirred, and gathered folds. Additional folds that enhance an illustration are those that show the action of the figure.

Choosing the right pose and angle to draw is critical in drawing the action folds since some views explain the action while others obscure it. If folds are formed around a figure and the figure is in motion we see places on the body called "source points," and folds form around these body areas. Gravity is the final fold principle. Evidence of folds formed by gravity can be seen in a long gown, where folds are formed from a garment line including the bust or waist. Many folds are non-essential and should be left out of the illustration in order to enhance the look of the clothing.

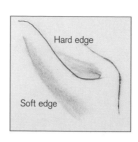

Fold example
This fold drawing (above) shows that on overlapping areas the line is hard and bold, while on planes that show width with no overlapping, the rendering is soft.

Rendered folds
This fold example (right) is showing fully rendered hard and soft fold edges. You can see that no folds are left out; each one is completely rendered. The model is draped in fabric that illustrates tucking, pinning, and knotting. These folds do not illustrate body action, yet they form around the figure in curved lines.

Line drawing
This line drawing illustrates only hard edges overlapping areas of the fold structure.

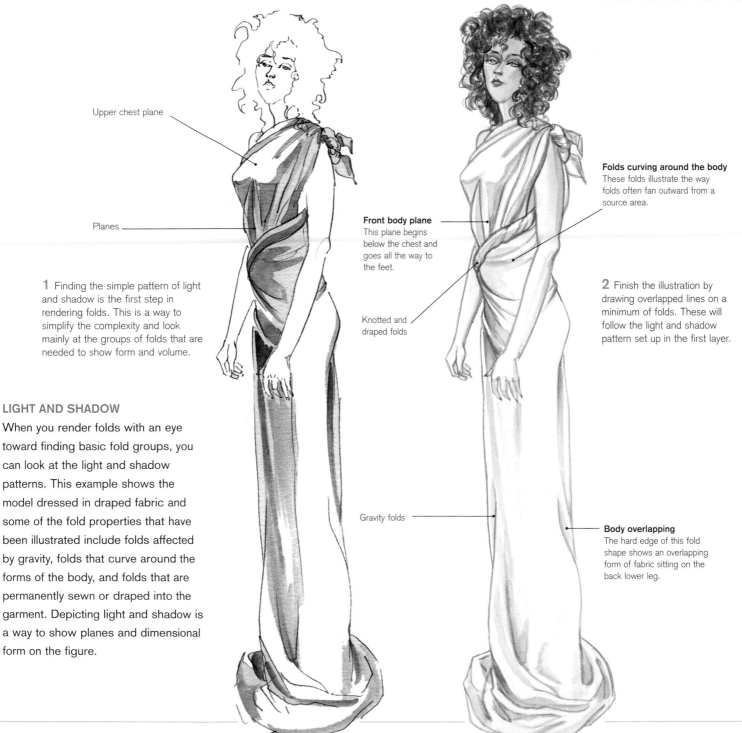

Upper chest plane

Planes

1 Finding the simple pattern of light and shadow is the first step in rendering folds. This is a way to simplify the complexity and look mainly at the groups of folds that are needed to show form and volume.

LIGHT AND SHADOW

When you render folds with an eye toward finding basic fold groups, you can look at the light and shadow patterns. This example shows the model dressed in draped fabric and some of the fold properties that have been illustrated include folds affected by gravity, folds that curve around the forms of the body, and folds that are permanently sewn or draped into the garment. Depicting light and shadow is a way to show planes and dimensional form on the figure.

Folds curving around the body
These folds illustrate the way folds often fan outward from a source area.

Front body plane
This plane begins below the chest and goes all the way to the feet.

Knotted and draped folds

2 Finish the illustration by drawing overlapped lines on a minimum of folds. These will follow the light and shadow pattern set up in the first layer.

Gravity folds

Body overlapping
The hard edge of this fold shape shows an overlapping form of fabric sitting on the back lower leg.

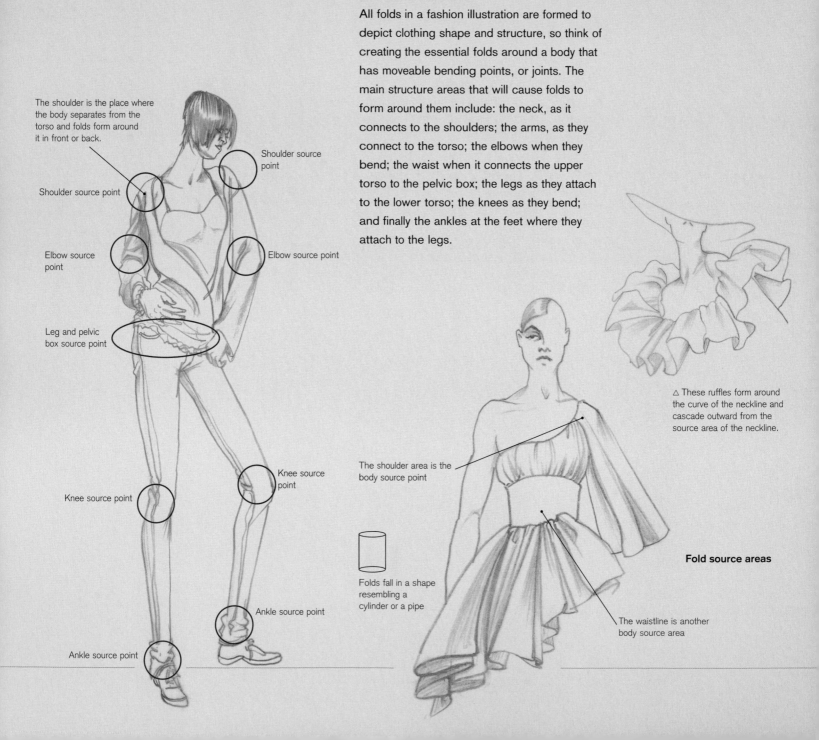

STRUCTURE POINTS

All folds in a fashion illustration are formed to depict clothing shape and structure, so think of creating the essential folds around a body that has moveable bending points, or joints. The main structure areas that will cause folds to form around them include: the neck, as it connects to the shoulders; the arms, as they connect to the torso; the elbows when they bend; the waist when it connects the upper torso to the pelvic box; the legs as they attach to the lower torso; the knees as they bend; and finally the ankles at the feet where they attach to the legs.

The shoulder is the place where the body separates from the torso and folds form around it in front or back.

Shoulder source point

Shoulder source point

Elbow source point

Elbow source point

Leg and pelvic box source point

Knee source point

Knee source point

Ankle source point

Ankle source point

△ These ruffles form around the curve of the neckline and cascade outward from the source area of the neckline.

The shoulder area is the body source point

Folds fall in a shape resembling a cylinder or a pipe

Fold source areas

The waistline is another body source area

ELBOW JOINT AND TYPICAL FOLD CONSTRUCTION

Folds that form around a joint are formed in the round. The view you select to draw will often show only part of the fold story. Here you can see that if you observe folds that form around the arm with a bend in the elbow, you can see the arm clearly showing beneath the fabric in some views while it is less obvious in other views. To fully grasp the complexity of fold drawing, think of making the folds appear to curve around forms, and draw them with a feeling of the figure under the clothing.

◁ **Side view—three-quarter back** ▷
The bend in the elbow causes folds to appear at the inner elbow and they curve around the entire area where the upper and lower arm are connected. Here, the folds start at the elbow and curve around the entire area of the joint. The fabric is thicker than the arm and sits outside of the arm line at the elbow.

◁ **Straight front view** ▷
Here is a typical fold situation where the arm has a bend in the elbow. You can see how the folds are forming near the inner elbow. The fabric has width and volume and sits on top of the body. The folds curve around the arm at the joint where the upper and lower arm connect.

◁ **Side view—three-quarter front** ▷
The folds are clearly sitting away from the body and are forming around the elbow. The folds are stretching from the elbow to the wrist in this view.

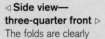 TURN THE PAGE For more folds and draping

Elbow source
Folds curve around the elbow.

Shoulder source
Here the shoulder shows the formation of folds behind the upper torso and curving around the shoulder.

Knee source
The knee is bent, and the model's lower right leg is in front of the upper part of the leg. The folds form behind the bend and curve around the knee.

Torso source
The folds are curving around the connection of the upper and lower torso at the waist and the beginning of the pelvic box.

Folds at the knee
Notice how the folds begin to drop from the model's left knee.

FOLDS AND BODY ACTION

Folds that show the body in action are illustrated on these pages. Every part of the body that can bend or twist does so in the pose illustrated on this page. The elbows are bent, the knees are bent, the torso is twisted between the upper part and the pelvic box and you can see evidence of the folds forming around all of the major body areas. The folds also show a lot of volume since they are constructed with width and thickness. The overlapping areas show hard-edge form and soft-edge rendering.

Stripes on fabric illustrate overlapping of folds
The places where the stripe curves under and reappears show that the fold overlap is a hard edge. The places where the stripe is clearly visible around the form are examples of fold rendering using soft edges.

FOLDS AND MOTION

When a model is walking, the fabric of a long dress flows outward in graceful curves. When you are illustrating a walking pose, the clothing needs to show the motion of the walk. This concept of drawing drapery to show movement will enhance the graceful appearance of your illustrations.

Source area: center front line and bust line
Folds drop from the center front line and the lower bust line.

Walking pose
The folds are moving down and backward because the model is walking forward.

Knee source point
Folds are dropping from the knee because the model is bending her leg. These folds cascade down and out in a triangular shaped form.

1 Gravity affects folds that drop from the bust line. The knee also causes some of these folds to drop from a source area. The fabric swings outward as the model moves forward.

2 The additional use of more vibrant color and outlines around the folds creates hard and soft folds that show volume and structure.

FOLDS AND FASHION

This drawing shows how folds can be created to curve around the figure, and the main group is formed around the pelvic box section. You can see one fold that curves between the model's left hip and her right knee. The entire group of folds that shows action of the pose fans out from the hip source point.

Simplifying folds

Fashion illustration is an art form that requires taking the concepts of a problem, like drawing and illustrating folds, and turning that problem into a simple and concise solution. The key is to retain the fold-drawing principles while making the folds appear beautiful, elegant, and graceful. The clothing you draw should look stylish and you will want to simplify all folds to show the body, the clothing details, and the structure of the folds you do draw.

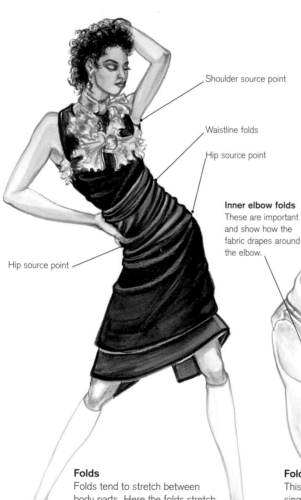

Shoulder source point

Waistline folds

Hip source point

Inner elbow folds
These are important and show how the fabric drapes around the elbow.

Hip source point

Hip source point

On the simplified version of the illustration, only one fold that starts at the shoulder and ends at the waist is needed.

In this example, **the** top contour edge of the sleeve is depicting the volume of the folds without overstating the overlapping of them.

Folds
Folds tend to stretch between body parts. Here the folds stretch between shoulder and hip, left hip and right hip, and hip and knee.

Folds and reality
This illustration shows how drawing every single fold can result in an overworked illustration. Here, the garment looks old, wrinkled, and unattractive.

Folds simplified
Here, many of the folds have been eliminated in favor of seeing the character of the fabric, the action of the pose, and the details of the garment.

CHOOSING WHAT TO INCLUDE

Remember that when you draw folds, you need to include the key folds that curve around, over, and across a body form. Understand where the overlapping edges are, indicate a hard and soft edge on the fold form, and simplify and eliminate folds for a more attractive illustration.

1 Dress the line drawing to indicate the main lines of the pose and show where the body is bending.

Folds caused by action of the body

Folds at shoulder and elbow

2 Draw the folds that are important to show the form of the figure and the action of the pose.

These folds form between the shoulder and the left hip.

Some folds are non-essential and are left out. Only show folds that will help you see a figure underneath and the action of the pose.

Note where the squeeze folds turn into stretch folds.

Minimizing the folds
Fashion illustration seeks to clarify the story of folds through careful editing of the non-essential ones. In this example you can see that the model is wearing a dress with folds that drop and curve down with gravity; they form a more interesting expression through minimalism.

Partial rendering
Try minimizing the detail in one part while enhancing it in another area. This partly rendered jacket is enough to show the structure of the garment, the choice of fabric, and the attitude of the figure—and the folds are complete without being overworked.

HATS

When you draw a hat, imagine you need to take a measurement of the head at the point where the hat would sit on top of the head. Hats need to be drawn to fit perfectly on the head and not be too loose or too tight; they touch the skull in several places. Most hats are composed of a brim and a crown, which can be shaped in a variety of ways. Hats might sit back on a head, to the side, or they may be pulled down low over the forehead. Observe the hat's placement on the head and create a stylish accessory every time you draw one.

TECHNIQUE

32 Accessories

Fashion accessories include bags, belts, shoes, socks, jewelry, hats, scarves, masks, ties, stockings, glasses, and gloves. You will need to be able to draw anything that combines with and enhances clothing. Observe details of accessories and explore how to use them to bring out the character of clothing. It is important to draw accessories with authority since they help to sell clothes and are tied into fashion in a big way.

The crown needs to fit the head and sit low enough so that the hat does not fly off the head with movement. The crown also needs to be larger than the head itself.

Brim
Shape the brim to fit the particular hat that you are drawing. This one has a curved shape that is placed on the model's head at a sideways angle.

Skull shape
Think about what the head looks like underneath both the hair and the hat.

Crown
In this view the hat is placed at an angle and is carefully constructed to show the correct style and fit.

Take care to draw the brim the same length on both sides.

SHOES

Shoes are detailed accessories, and work well when they are placed onto the model's feet with an understanding of the underlying anatomical structure. Illustrating shoes requires you to look for the shape of the shoe, the angle of the shoe from the toe to the heel, and the detailing. Observe and draw the shape of the toe of the shoe, illustrate the heel, and look for the place where the planes change directions. The outside part of the shoe is always wider than the inside part.

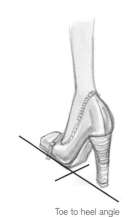

Toe to heel angle

△ Side view
This view is easy, and in a heel you will see a negative space between the toe and the heel of the shoe.

Shoe structure
In this example, the shoe lines curve around the foot.

Profile view

Toe to heel angle

Vertical line
This line establishes the heel.

Shoe width
Shoes are wider on the outside edge.

Plane change area
The foot starts arching under the boot at this point.

▽ Center guideline
Drawing a line in the middle of the shoe and foot creates a guideline that is helpful in seeing the way the outside half of the shoe is wider than the inside half.

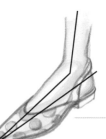

Seam lines
The cut of the boots and the seams of the leather provide areas where the form can be seen to curve and reveal the underlying shape of the foot.

Toe to heel angle

▭▷ **TURN THE PAGE** For more accessories

MEN'S SHOES

Drawing men's shoes requires an awareness of planes. When a curved form changes direction and can be illustrated by seeing a flat surface, you have a plane. In an illustration context, a plane is a flat surface that can be rendered in a darker value to show angularity. Men's shoes have a structure that is higher at the front opening than in the back. The view from the underside of a man's shoe shows how the outside half is wider than the inside half.

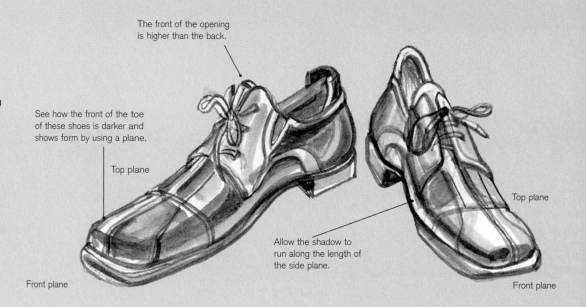

The front of the opening is higher than the back.

See how the front of the toe of these shoes is darker and shows form by using a plane.

Top plane

Front plane

Top plane

Allow the shadow to run along the length of the side plane.

Front plane

▽ **Look at the shape**
The view of the shoe from underneath shows the shape of the shoe and how the toe is curved toward one side. If you drew a center line down the middle of the shoe you would see the way the outside edge of the shoe is longer than the inside edge.

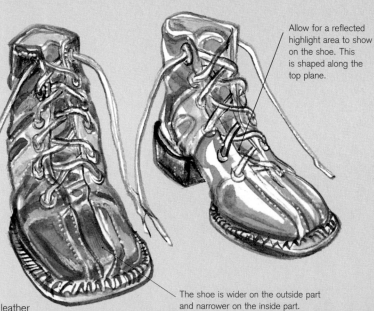

This illustrates where the widest parts of the shoe are located. The outside part of the shoe is wider than the inside part.

▷ **Details**
The curves of both shoelaces, leather inserts, and the cut lines of the center of the shoe can help to show form.

Allow for a reflected highlight area to show on the shoe. This is shaped along the top plane.

The shoe is wider on the outside part and narrower on the inside part.

JEWELRY

Rings are worn as a symbol of wealth. Historically they have been around since the days of ancient Egypt and Greece. They appear on all fingers and show distinctive styling. To illustrate the specifics of detail required in rendering any form of jewelry, it is important to look at shape and color of the pieces you wish to render. Metallic pigments can be used to render gold and silver jewelry or you can illustrate the value contrast changes with paint in multiple values. If there are precious stones in the jewelry, you will need multiple values of a color and highlights of white. Use bracelets, necklaces, distinctive pins, belts, and all other kinds of accessory jewelry to enhance your fashion illustrations.

Value contrast
Create light and dark value in a base color for more glowing effects with metallic surfaces.

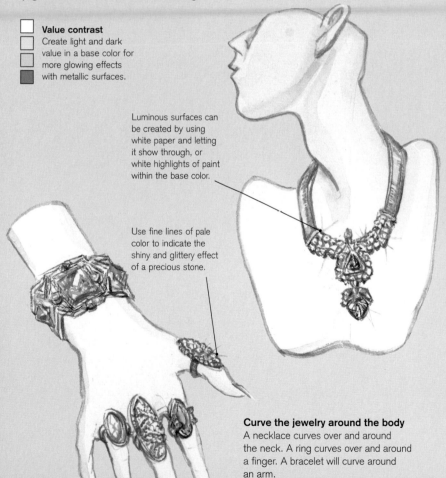

Luminous surfaces can be created by using white paper and letting it show through, or white highlights of paint within the base color.

Use fine lines of pale color to indicate the shiny and glittery effect of a precious stone.

Curve the jewelry around the body
A necklace curves over and around the neck. A ring curves over and around a finger. A bracelet will curve around an arm.

BAGS

Bags can be used to show style and are a popular luxury accessory. All sizes of bags made from a wide variety of materials are part of fashion illustration so learn to draw the details, silhouette shape, and the texture of each type of bag—including paper shopping bags.

Value contrast
Use highlights and draw several values into the main color. This example uses a white highlight on parts of the bag and a pale yellow/orange with a darker orange and an even darker red/orange. The color and value can change simultaneously.

Texture
If the bag is leather, draw a surface pattern over the top of the base color to give a more grainy appearance to the surface of the rendering.

Shape
Bags come in all sizes and shapes. Work on showing the angle and symmetry when you draw the shape of the bag. Avoid a lack of structure and form.

▷ TURN THE PAGE For more accessories

OTHER ACCESSORIES

The key to completing great accessories is to layer the illustration. Begin with a drawing, add layers of color and details, and then move onto the finished piece by completing the outlines around the illustrations. The use of details and the additional time taken to complete accessories will be worth the effort since each piece adds to the mood and drama of the final example.

◁ **Fun details**
The cute socks and color-matched bag and wedge sandals complement this fun outfit.

◁ **Bold color**
Here, the vibrant stockings and shoes make a statement. No other accessories are needed.

▷ **Buckle**
In this minimal illustration, the belt buckle provides a focus.

△ **Belt**
Curve the form of the belt around the figure, based on the eye level and the "smile" and "frown" concepts (see page 76).

◁ **Necktie**
Create folds and volume by using highlights and use pattern and texture as needed.

◁ **Decorative mask**
This is an example of an accessory that has so much detail that you will need to create a simple color on the face and less detail in the makeup effects to balance it.

▷ **Stockings**
Draw stockings to show form and volume. Avoid the flatness that can occur with colors over forms by making the value contrast of one darker than the other and creating darker value on the sides of the stockings.

Try working on a variety of garment types to learn more about illustrating the silhouette shape and all of the proportional relationships you need to understand to illustrate and draw fashion. You can use the many styles in this chapter to practice your mapping skills.

Experiment with mapping garments onto a figure you have prepared—this will be easier if you see a few types of garments that have a wide variety of silhouette shapes. Remember to consider what each garment might be constructed out of and factor that into your practice as you draw and design specific garment types.

5

Garment Types

Tops

The wide variety of tops and shirts is not a problem in illustration since drawing techniques are based upon the key lines and points of the garment, and mapping these onto a figure. Shirts can be loose-fitting or fitted, and can have sleeves or be sleeveless. Draw the structure lines of the shirt by placing the seams carefully, and create enough space in armholes to allow for the figure's movement.

Fitted leisure shirt
This garment contours the body for a fitted shape that combines with the side splits and double rows of top stitching to create a sporty feel.

Kaftan top
A less fitted shape that skims the body. The embroidered border frames the notch-cut neckline as well as emphasizing the three-quarter length sleeves.

Hooded sweat top
A sporty look that should drape around the body in a relaxed fit. Note the ribbed trims and double top-stitching.

Bustier
This garment should cling to the body and support it, emphasizing the curves. Try combining it with a looser fitting top or skirt for a great contrast.

Halter-neck handkerchief top
The fitted upper section of this top combines with the fluid gathers below. Try including some movement in the figure, to show off the asymmetric hem.

Wrapover belted cardigan
A relaxed garment to drape around the figure. Knitwear must look bulky without being frumpy. Your figure might hold the garment open to reveal what is worn beneath.

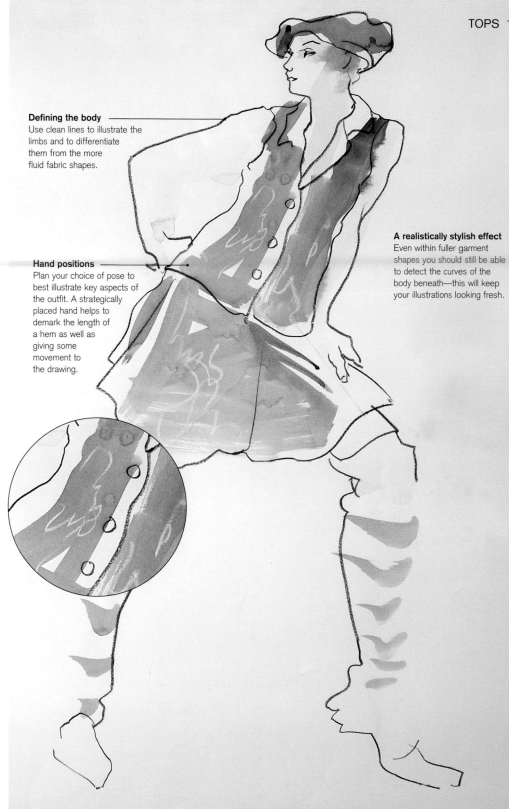

Defining the body
Use clean lines to illustrate the limbs and to differentiate them from the more fluid fabric shapes.

Hand positions
Plan your choice of pose to best illustrate key aspects of the outfit. A strategically placed hand helps to demark the length of a hem as well as giving some movement to the drawing.

A realistically stylish effect
Even within fuller garment shapes you should still be able to detect the curves of the body beneath—this will keep your illustrations looking fresh.

Classic blouse
A semi-fitted shape that is given fullness by emphasizing the gathers at the yoke and cuffs. Try a gentle folded bow for a classic look or a pussy bow for a sexy retro feel.

Classic woven shirt
A fitted shape and curved hem to mold around the figure. Woven fabric will have a stiffer appearance than jersey and will not cling to the body in the same way.

Skirts

Skirt drawing is dependent upon the type of skirt you are creating. A simple straight skirt follows the form of the legs. Draw the folds wider at the base and allow them to flow with gravity and motion. The form of the hem will be determined by the skirt's cut and the pose action. Locate the knees and allow the folds to form around them. If the fabric is thin, there will be sharper folds. If the skirt has lots of detail, make the pose simpler to accentuate the garment.

Five-pocket Western styling
This skirt will be fitted to the body but will retain a gentle A-line silhouette due to fabric stiffness. The double row of top stitching is a form of jeans styling.

Handkerchief hem skirt
Choose a pose with maximum movement for this type of skirt. Allow the skirt to kick out with a raised leg or swish of the hips to clearly illustrate that all-important hemline.

Wrapover tie-front skirt
This is an elegant garment that requires a simple pose. Drape the folds around the legs so that they remain defined, and with movement some leg may be revealed.

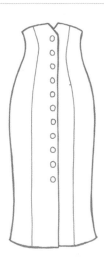

Corset skirt
A fitted garment that follows and molds the shape of the body beneath. Any over garment will need to be illustrated open, so as not to lose the dramatic effect.

Gathered pleats
This skirt varies depending on the choice of fabric. In a stiff satin those folds will jut out aggressively, while in a soft washed cotton they will follow the contours of the legs.

Gypsy skirt
Tiers of gathers form an A-line shape. This is the perfect skirt to place on an active figure with a great deal of movement so that all of those frills can swish away to great effect.

Movement within artwork
When applying color to your illustration, ensure that the direction of your marks is sympathetic to the direction of the fabric for a more natural effect.

Puffball
This is a difficult shape—it can appear unflattering as the gathers create a lot of volume, and the figure can be lost. Clearly define the hip points and use a fun pose.

Knife pleats
This is always going to be a formal look requiring classic styling. Use movement to make the pleats kick out from where the top stitching ends to the bottom edge of the hem.

The body beneath
Never lose sight of those all-important points where the garment maps over the shape of the body.

Pleats and folds
Remember that light colors will appear naturally highlighted, and that darker tones will recess backward. The shadows within folds can be emphasized using a range of gray shades to give greater depth to your illustration.

Hemline
The contour of the hemline is very important in defining the nature of the pleats within the skirt—the sharper the pleats, the straighter the folds at the hem.

Pants

35

When drawing pants, remember the concept of the pelvic box—fit the pants at the hip and construct them around the figure. Draw the pants using the center front line, the center back line, and all details of pockets, cuffs, and folds in the illustration to show a body underneath. Remember to overlap forms correctly, and place the front form over the back at the center front and back. The fabric and pants are constructed to fit the hips and flare outward, forming a wide variety of shapes in the pant legs.

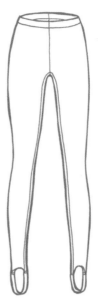

Ski pants
These fit the legs all the way to the ankle, clearly showing the body beneath. Made from jersey, they stretch around the figure.

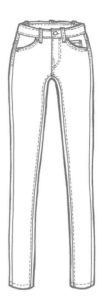

Five-pocket Western styling
These pants have a skinny fit. By varying the fit from the knee they can be adapted to a bootleg cut or even a true 70s flare.

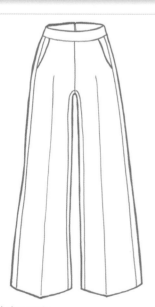

Wide-leg pants
The flare begins at the hips, creating a lovely fluid line. This garment demands a pose with movement to best show it off.

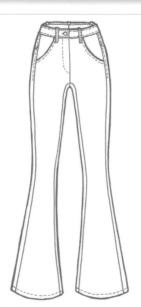

Killer flares
Pants with attitude that demand a suitable pose. The line flares stiffly from the knee, especially in heavyweight denim fabric.

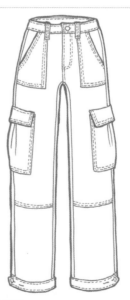

Cargo pants
Keep the pose simple so that you can show all of the details. Reference the knees within the drapes to ensure a stylish effect.

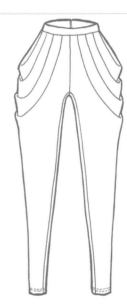

Harem pants
Have fun with the exotically draping layers. Be careful with your choice of shoe; simple styles best complement this complex silhouette.

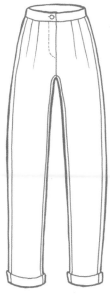

Chinos
A classic but relaxed style. Make the hip and knee points clear or this garment can look a little stodgy on the figure.

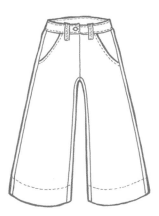

Bermuda shorts
Shorts are increasingly used in heavier fabrics for winter styling. Flare them from the hip and clearly describe their length by denoting the hem in relation to the knee.

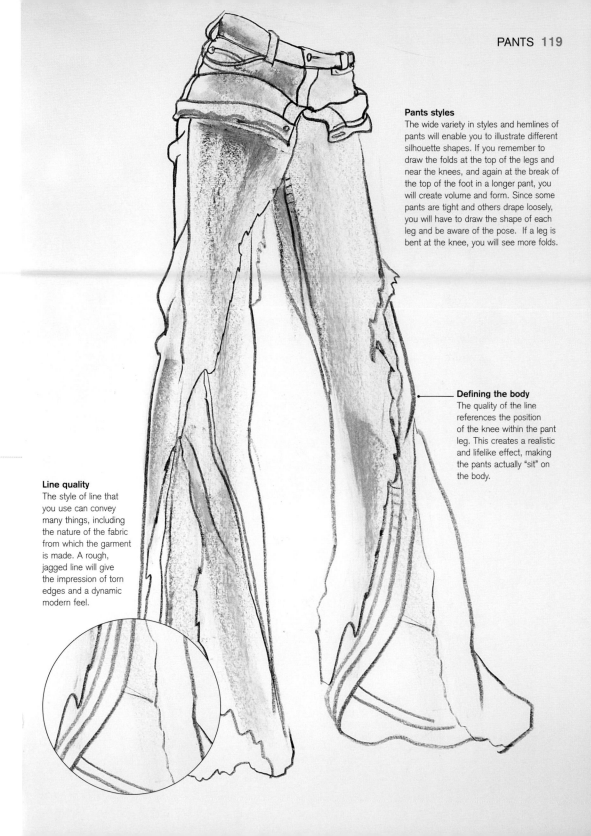

Pants styles
The wide variety in styles and hemlines of pants will enable you to illustrate different silhouette shapes. If you remember to draw the folds at the top of the legs and near the knees, and again at the break of the top of the foot in a longer pant, you will create volume and form. Since some pants are tight and others drape loosely, you will have to draw the shape of each leg and be aware of the pose. If a leg is bent at the knee, you will see more folds.

Defining the body
The quality of the line references the position of the knee within the pant leg. This creates a realistic and lifelike effect, making the pants actually "sit" on the body.

Line quality
The style of line that you use can convey many things, including the nature of the fabric from which the garment is made. A rough, jagged line will give the impression of torn edges and a dynamic modern feel.

Jackets

The main principle to remember when drawing a jacket is to lengthen the model's neck. Sometimes the collar can obscure the view of the neck, and if you draw the head too close to the shoulders, the illustration can appear awkward. The jacket is a garment that can fit loosely over the figure, or it can be fitted. Remember to look for all the key lines, and use your knowledge of folds to heighten the elbow's bending capability.

Cropped jacket
Lengthening the neck of the figure allows space to show off the large collar. The single button will be a point of tension between both sides of the garment.

Formal fitted jacket
The sleeves of this jacket fold tightly around the arms. Although fitted to the body, the line flares out slightly from the hip. Include seam lines to emphasize the shape of the body.

Jeans jacket
This is a very familiar style of jacket. Even if you do not depict every detail within your drawing the viewer will easily understand the kind of garment that you are portraying.

Military style jacket
The boxy shoulders and double-breasted styling give this jacket a formal appearance. This, combined with the banding on the cuffs, creates a stylish military look.

Scooped collar
The plunging collar on this jacket creates a feminine effect. It drapes over the body and any garments beneath. If the jacket is the star of the show, keep the outfit simple.

Tracksuit jacket
This is an unmistakably casual garment with its raglan sleeves, zips, and stand-up collar. The ribbed hem hugs the hips but the rest of the fabric will drape around the body.

Safari jacket
This is a casual garment, but the belted
waist adds shape and defines the body.
Choose a simple pose to show the details
of the pockets and top-stitching.

Biker jacket
The stiffer the fabric or leather of this
jacket, the fewer the folds around the waist
and elbows of the figure. A simple pose
allows focus on styling details.

Drape over the body
Place seam lines to emphasize
the fit of the jacket over the body
as it curves into the waist and over
the hips.

Tight-fitting jacket
When the jacket fits the body more closely,
it is important to form the curving garment
construction lines around the form of the figure.
The seams will enable you to draw the fitted jacket
with authority. Pay attention to the center front
opening on a jacket and the line of the torso in the
pose. If the body is jutting forward in a side pose,
the front line will show this angle.

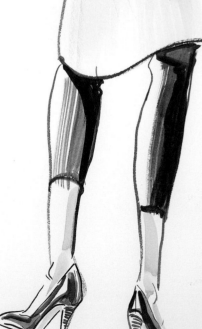

Rendering lines
Use the direction of
rendering lines to emphasize
the drape of the fabric in
the jacket. Major seams
will follow the angle of
the shoulders and hips of
the figure.

Coats

A coat needs to fully cover the figure in a voluminous manner and is likely to be textured. Ask yourself: Is the fabric shiny, rough-textured, smooth, or grainy in appearance? Dry brush is the perfect technique for many richly textured fabrics. A textured paper can also help. The illustration will be enhanced by the paper grade. Illustrate the mood and look of the garment by depicting a strong attitude with your model's pose and a garment laden with texture details.

Funnel neck
This coat is a wide shape—the body needs to be suggested beneath in order for it not to appear shapeless. A front view would best illustrate the one-sided pocket detail.

Pea coat
A fitted style that flares from the hip. Elongate the neck of the figure to allow space for the complicated collar. Choose a pose to show the double-breasted fastening clearly.

Trench coat
This is a classic style of coat. The belt is a great device for making the garment appear to rest on the body. With movement the hem of the coat will swing out.

Princess-line coat
The collar drapes across the shoulders, held in tension by the outer button. Remember to show the parallel seaming as this is an important feature of the design.

Duffel coat
A classic style, generally made from a very solid cloth. A hand-on-hip pose allows for more shape and interesting styling. A rear-view illustration would show the hood.

Quilted casual coat
This jacket skims the body and there is a wonderful contrast of texture between the soft quilting and the fur-lined hood. Show all of the gathers around the bands of stitching.

Fully rendered coat
This coat has a fitted appearance, and the surface texture looks shiny. It's rendered to emphasize the model's stylish and sexy attitude. This drawing shows the way the form of the fabric fits over the body. The waist is belted and the hem follows the hip angle. The collar is fit around the body, and the model's long neck makes this fit look stylish. This pose is selected to illustrate the coat to its best advantage. The hem suggests motion as the model walks forward.

Hand position
Placing a hand on the hips ensures that the shape of the figure can be clearly seen beneath the volume of the coat. This creates a more sensual effect and underlines the style of the garment.

Defining the pelvis
The position of the second hand means that the angle of the hips can be clearly understood. This adds to the sense of movement within the drawing as well as making the garment appear to rest on the body. You can almost see those pompoms flinging themselves in the air as the figure turns.

Sporty raincoat
The dynamic seam lines and fabric inserts create a sporty feel and your choice of pose should reflect this. Pull-tabs on the pockets create a sense of movement.

Fur coat
A dry paint brush will capture the fur effect with lots of energetic brush strokes. Have fun with the pose—draping the coat over the shoulders or depicting it open with something fabulous underneath.

Dresses

A dress looks best with a simple pose so that the garment details are the main focus. The dress is designed to be a body-enhancing garment, and as such, it will attract attention. The illustration should accentuate the figure and sexuality of the model. The skirt swing should show when the model walks. When the skirt hangs straight with no figure movement, pay attention to the width of the hemline and notice how the silhouette forms around the body. For an evening gown, the legs may not show, so make sure the figure has the correct proportions.

Babydoll dress
This is a cute style of dress, so style your model accordingly. The line of the hips and resulting leg positions are vital, so that the body is not lost within the gathers of fabric.

Tube dress
This garment has very little movement on the body, and will not swing as the model walks, because it is closely fitted to the figure at both the bust and hemlines.

Bias-cut dress
The draping neckline, diagonal seaming and fluted hem show that this dress is cut on the bias. Let your fabric softly flow over the body and go for a demure pose.

Wraparound dress
The appearance of this style will very much depend upon the fabric from which it is constructed. A soft jersey, for instance, will result in a fluid, draped effect.

Kimono
This simple garment is given shape by the use of the wide tie belt. There is great volume in the upper body and the stiffness of the fabric dictates how the sleeves hang.

Shirt dress
The shoulder line is emphasized by the seaming, and the waistline by the belt. Create a smooth line with plenty of movement where the hem line kicks away from the waist.

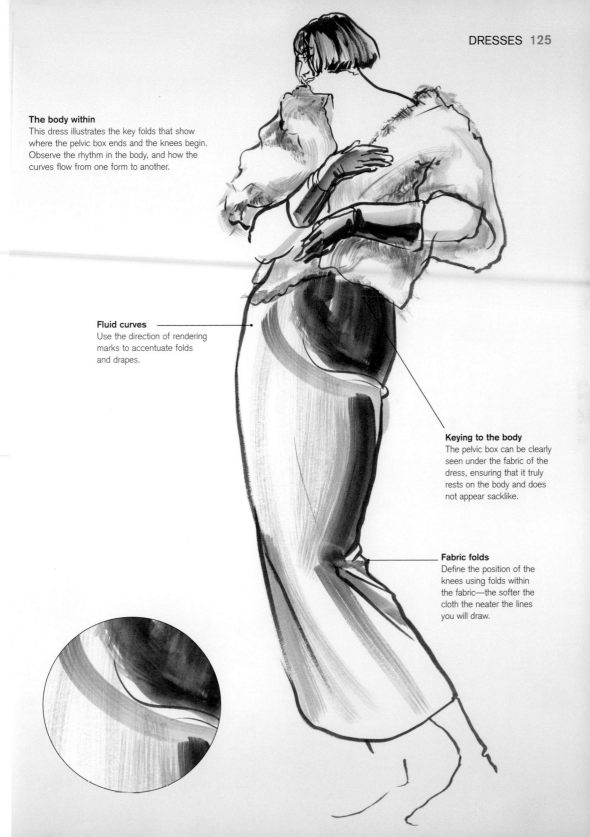

The body within
This dress illustrates the key folds that show where the pelvic box ends and the knees begin. Observe the rhythm in the body, and how the curves flow from one form to another.

Fluid curves
Use the direction of rendering marks to accentuate folds and drapes.

Keying to the body
The pelvic box can be clearly seen under the fabric of the dress, ensuring that it truly rests on the body and does not appear sacklike.

Fabric folds
Define the position of the knees using folds within the fabric—the softer the cloth the neater the lines you will draw.

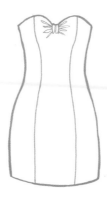

Strapless fitted dress
This garment relies on a neat fit to hold it up. The line of the model should be seen both in silhouette and in the way in which the seams follow the contours of the body.

Smocked style
The smocking is a fantastic texture that hugs the body, then all of that fabric is released into an abundance of gathers. Go for a dynamic pose to accentuate the volume.

Once you have mastered mapping the various garment types onto your figure, you will want to render them to give an impression of the fabric they are made from. Fabrics respond to light in different ways and this gives each a unique character. Try to capture the tactile qualities of fabrics in your illustrations—the techniques on the following pages show you how to achieve this for many of the main fabric types you will be depicting.

CHAPTER

6

Fabric

Rendering basics

All successful fashion illustrations involve fabric rendering. You can learn how to render the surface characteristics as you observe the smoothness or roughness of fabrics. The following pages show how to illustrate and simplify the rendering of many fabrics—this will enhance your ability to simplify and illustrate your croquis figures.

ILLUSTRATION METHODOLOGY

One characteristic of all illustrations is that they are produced in layers. This process of drawing a layered illustration requires you to find and draw a croquis figure (see page 48). You must then transfer this figure to a painting surface, making decisions about media and process as you go. There are two basic ways to render: one is to color every part of the drawing and complete all the details of the illustration at once. The second way is to draw parts of the figure and paint these parts separately.

▷ **Sparing out white**
This illustration is an example of "sparing out white," where a lot of the white paper remains unpainted. The strengths of the fully rendered style are that you can be more realistic and illustrate all aspects of the fabric textures. The drawback of the fully rendered style is that it is slower to execute. The "sparing out white" style, on the other hand, has brevity and looseness as its strong points, while clarity of details is a drawback.

◁ **Capturing a
shiny surface**
The folds in this satin dress
create a rhythm of light and
shade across the folds of
the fabric. Light colors will
always jump forward to
create highlights while
darker shades recede to
form shadows.

◁ **Rough texture**
Knitted garments are often chunky,
especially when handknitted or made
on heavy gauge machinery. Do not be
daunted—this represents a fantastic
opportunity for you to experiment with
different textures. Try out dry paint, old
marker pens, collage—have fun trying
to represent what you see on the
surface of the fabric.

◁ **Dynamic contrasts**
Rendering comes into its own
where you have an outfit that
combines contrasting textures
and colors. The high shine of
the boots and corset shown
here are perfectly set off by the
linear patterning of the fishnet
leggings, while the touch of
color at the bust finishes the
composition off.

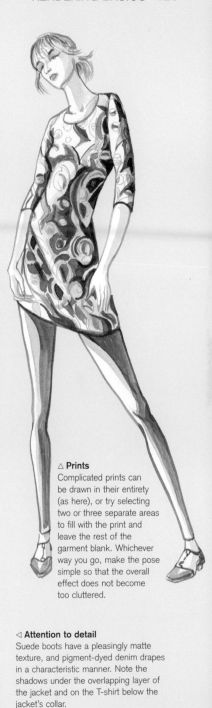

△ **Prints**
Complicated prints can
be drawn in their entirety
(as here), or try selecting
two or three separate areas
to fill with the print and
leave the rest of the
garment blank. Whichever
way you go, make the pose
simple so that the overall
effect does not become
too cluttered.

◁ **Attention to detail**
Suede boots have a pleasingly matte
texture, and pigment-dyed denim drapes
in a characteristic manner. Note the
shadows under the overlapping layer of
the jacket and on the T-shirt below the
jacket's collar.

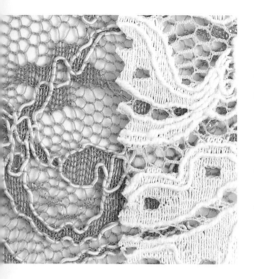

LACE

Lace will show transparent effects so you will need to draw the base color of the form under the lace. Think about this color: if you see a body color under the lace, use a flesh-toned layer on the first color gradation. Lace is a pattern of flowers, leaves, or other shapes. Determine the pattern and draw each leaf or flower.

Place crosshatched lines between the pattern elements—this can be done with a felt-tipped pen or a gouache paint color mixed to match the color of the lace. Use a small brush to paint the lace pattern. To get form and dimension in your illustration, draw the background lace shape with light and dark value.

△ **Lace rendering**
This illustration shows the main lace-drawing concepts, including the drawing of a ground color under the lace.

Step 1
As a transparent fabric, lace will appear to float over any surfaces that can be seen beneath. This will depend upon the outfit that you are illustrating. Your base layer below the lace should be more subtle than any areas of the garment or skin seen without lace covering them.

Step 2
Lace is a very variable material, ranging from an extremely delicate structure to a very textural and chunky fabric. Try to evoke the true nature of your particular lace paying special attention to scale in relation to the figure. You can either fill the space with texture or be selective about rendering two or three areas only.

Step 3
Place a wash of a generalized mesh effect over the top for the final layer, trying to avoid the areas that were previously left white. This will prevent the piece being overworked. Use a precise drawing implement such as a sharp colored pencil for a light and fine effect.

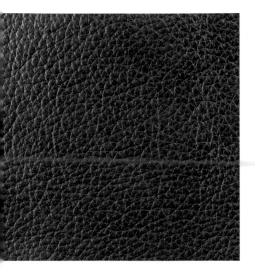

LEATHER

Reflective surfaces show more range of value contrast—you can draw leather with all nine values in the scale. To show the character of the surface texture, plan to create a coarse, grainy effect over the surface of the color. Draw a thin shape of highlight that will run along the side of your form.

This shape will spare out the white on your illustration. Complete the rendering by adding a black prismacolor pencil line around the forms to sharpen the outline of the shape. Then take a white prismacolor pencil and apply texture to the top of the highlight shape. Remember that leather is a thick, coarse fabric and will show up well as a bold, thick fold structure.

Step 1
When building up the rendering layers for leather consider how matte or shiny your fabric appears to be. Nearly all leathers have a high degree of subtle texture. White paper allowed to show through close to the seams will become bright highlights—suggesting a thick and stiff fabric.

Step 2
Adding darker tones of marker pen, creates a deeper, more luxurious effect and suggests a nap in the leather. These darker marks also serve to make the white highlights appear even more contrasting and accentuated.

Step 3
The final addition of a very subtle layer of soft black pencil pulls the whole range of colors together. This layer further enforces an appearance of fine texture on the surface of the leather—making this jacket an unmistakably solid outerwear garment.

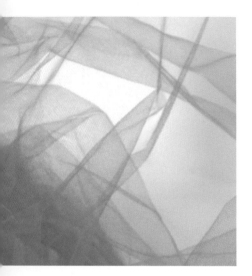

TRANSPARENT EFFECTS

Many fabrics have a transparent effect and you can see through them. Draw them by completing the background color first and then applying the transparent layer over it. Chiffon, tulle, and lace are examples of fabrics that are sheer. Create a wash over the shape of the fabric after applying the background color. In areas not covering the body use a light value wash.

Use darker washes for overlapping folds. The transparent fabric is often covering another fabric. In this case the value will be affected by the color and value of the overlapping sheer fabric. Each medium is slightly different in approach, but all techniques demand the application of layers.

△ **Layered effect**
The chiffon illustration shows the layering required to see the background body and clothing colors through the chiffon. After rendering the body and pants, the chiffon was illustrated using a white gouache paint mixture thinned down and painted over the shape of the draped fabric.

STEP 1
The challenge of rendering transparent fabrics is to balance what can be seen through the fabric with the appearance of the material itself. Sheer fabrics are lightweight and so you must avoid the temptation to overwork the drawing or the effect will become too stodgy. Less is more, so be selective and brave enough to leave plenty of white areas of paper showing through.

STEP 2
When rendering a transparent material use a transparent form of color and build up layers of the same medium—allowing each layer to dry thoroughly between each application. Inks are perfect for this task, but marker pens and watered down paints can be very effective also.

STEP 3
Concentrate the color in areas of shadows within folds and where a number of layers of the transparent fabric are seen overlapping each other. A single layer over skin will be the palest area and is best left as a single wash of color. If the effect is starting to look over worked, stop, evaluate, and add dry white pencil to highlighted areas if necessary to bring the drawing back to life.

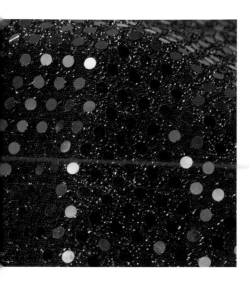

SEQUINS

Sparkle fabric textures are created in a similar way to tulle fabric (see page 132). The use of markers and a piece of tulle fabric will provide the first layer of color. This dotted layer of color is then enhanced using a gel pen. Special effects are applied, using a line to indicate shine and creating it on individual sequins by drawing a star-shaped highlight. Look also for a thin highlight shape that runs the full length of the body. Leave this highlight white.

▷ **Showing shine**
Note the star-shaped lines in this dress. These are the special effects that are used to show a shiny surface.

STEP 1
First, establish the base color. This has been applied in watery bands rather than as a plain wash. The final textural effect is suggested but does not yet evoke a sparkling appearance.

STEP 2
A darker tone comes next with a stippled pattern of dots. Try to avoid covering the entire garment with this texture. The blurred effect begins to evoke a feeling of sequins.

STEP 3
Finally, the highlights. Look at the shape and scale of the sequins, as well as how densely they are applied. Add highlights on the areas nearest the viewer with a sharp soft pencil.

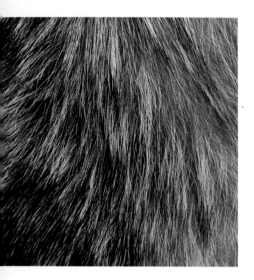

FUR

Fur is composed of hair, and must be drawn to show its character—whether the hair is long, short, or curled. Fur garments are heavy and they drape with thick folds. Fur is a softly textured fabric that you can easily render by blending washes of watercolor. Use two values and wet-in-wet techniques with watercolor application. Add lines over the wash as a second layer. These may be created in pencil, charcoal, or pastel. The contour outlines of fur should be non-enclosed outlines that illustrate the individual hairs.

△ This fur collar shows how the fur curves around the neck and creates a heavy, yet soft and textured look.

STEP 1

Representing the texture of fur begins with the style of the line used before the rendering even begins. Follow this same style of linear texture as the first layer of color is put down. Darker tones are placed where shadows naturally fall to begin to build up a sense of volume.

STEP 2

Use a tonal range of colors that reflect the true color of the fur and blend together effectively. Many tones combined together give a greater feeling of depth to the texture of the fur. Soft pencil has been used here to evoke a sense of the softness in the fur.

STEP 3

Ensure that some areas are left white for the paper to show through. Fur has a sheen that creates fine highlights within the texture of the garment. The original outline can still be seen—this keeps the drawing from looking over-colored and retains a light, stylish appearance.

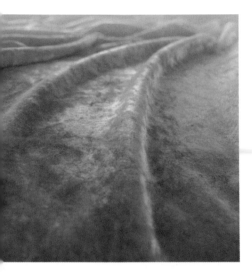

VELVET

Velvet reflects very little light, and this means that your illustration will contain a minimal number of values, and the edges where light and shadow meet should be soft. Tones can be blended while the paint is wet using colored ink or watercolor. This will give you a blurred look reminiscent of velvet surface texture. Apply light and dark pastel or colored pencils over the washes to get more richness of texture. Pencil texture provides a way to blend the colors from the first layer together and bring out the soft gradations.

△ **Soft texture**
Note the soft shading used on this rendering of velvet. The matte finish of the surface texture and the soft blending complete the illusion of velvet fabric.

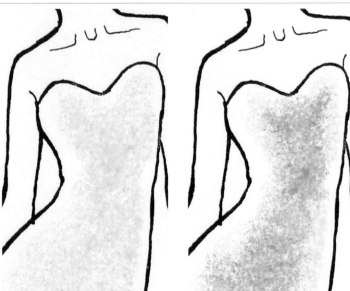

STEP 1
Apply the first layer of color with a textured sponge or stippling brush for maximum tonal variation. This layer will be blended at later stages and so the greater the depth of texture at this stage, the more interesting the final effect will be.

STEP 2
Adjust the base color until it is an accurate representation of your fabric. Don't worry about allowing these layers to fully dry out between applications since the desired effect is of a blended appearance. Keep the tonal variation at this stage.

STEP 3
Finally blend all of the other layers, allowing them to bleed together—use a very clean brush with a controlled wash of water. Don't allow your drawing to get too messy—stay in control. Once dry, add a highlight of soft white pencil to accentuate the figure.

TEXTURE

Rough-textured fabrics include tweed and bouclé. They can be rendered by applying a layer of color, using markers or watercolor. Allow a little white paper to show through as you cover the shape with color to keep the illustration fresh and vibrant. Experiment with using textured paper when you apply your media.

Notice that there are scattered flecks of color over a tweed fabric surface. Add these with colored pencils. Bouclé fabric has a woven texture with scattered bits of color. To get the right fabric surface appearance use gouache paint over a layer of watercolor. Paint the dots of texture on top of the first layer using a small brush.

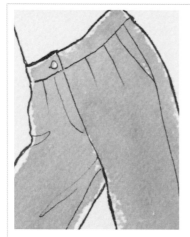

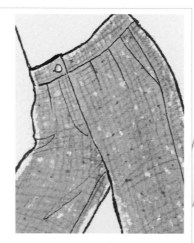

STEP 1

Keep in mind that you are going to be layering up your textural effects, and begin with a base wash of solid color, such as watercolor. By using the layering method, each part can be allowed to dry to avoid a confusing mess. Allowing brush strokes to be seen results in a more exciting outcome.

STEP 2

Now think about adding the main texture. Don't overwork your design, and remember to leave those areas of white paper showing through that looked so good in Step 1, for a fresher feel. A soft pencil has been used here to define the weave of the cloth, suggesting shadows within the texture.

STEP 3

Look again at the fabric that you are trying to represent. Have fun experimenting with dabs of color or stippling white accents to really bring the surface to life. Try different materials out on spare paper such as gouache, ink, or wax crayons. Concentrate this last layer more heavily on the areas closer to the viewer to act as a highlight.

△ **Bouclé suit**
The base color was applied, followed by a second layer where a small brush with white opaque gouache was used to dry-brush the paint onto the illustration.

KNITS

Knitwear is interesting both in silhouette and texture. There is a wide variety of complexity of knits—some knits can look almost sculptural. Create most of the texture on the knit on the top layer. Experiment with covering the entire illustration with the stitch texture, or try a more minimal approach by drawing the stitches on the place where light and shadow meet. Try drawing a knit garment on a rough-textured paper. The "tooth" of the paper will help you create the texture you need with minimal effort. Draw the contour lines that appear on the edges of the knit with a bumpy line quality.

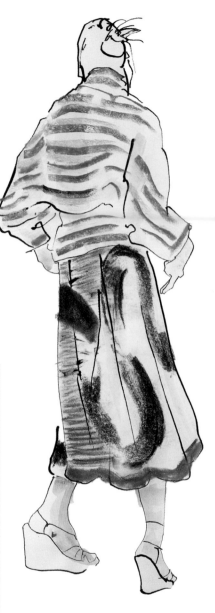

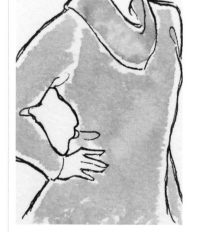

STEP 1
Marker pen over textured watercolor paper gives a sense of volume. Notice that the areas left white for the paper to show through are just as important as those filled with color.

STEP 2
A smudgy chalk pastel has been used to add further texture, depth, and movement. The darker pastel also adds shadows. The smudged edges help to suggest soft cashmere knitwear.

STEP 3
The knit stitches are rendered in pencil. The texture is carefully placed —fully fashioning marks around the armholes, for instance. Too much texture could look too chainmail-like.

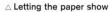

△ **Letting the paper show**
The colors were placed over the drawing with dry pastel. Look at the way the white paper is spared out and how the pastel was applied to give the impression of texture and form.

DENIM

Denim is a rough-textured fabric. Think about its weight and texture when you illustrate it. There is a wide variety of denim colors, so create a color swatch before working directly on the illustration.

When illustrating denim, apply the color in the first layer roughly, with a scrubbing motion; an abrupt and non-smooth stroke that shows the character of the thick fabric. After the base color dries, apply thin lines with a white colored pencil in the direction of the fabric's grain or weft. Gold stitching can be applied with a small brush and gouache paint, or a gel pen. The use of a thicker piece of paper with a rough surface texture is one way to get the look of denim.

△ **Explore different media**
Experiment with paper and media, and come up with the formula that works for you. Here, the artist uses watercolor, letting the white of the paper show through.

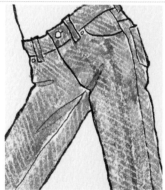

STEP 1
The base layer of color is applied with rough strokes parallel to the direction of the outlines of the jeans. This results in a sense of energy and movement without the overall effect becoming too messy. Note the areas of white paper beneath that have been allowed to show through.

STEP 2
Adding the diagonal texture leaves the viewer in no doubt that these pants are made from denim. Examining a piece of this fabric in reality will reveal that it has a slanting linear construction or twill. The white pencil marks suggest highlights resting on the twill.

STEP 3
Attention to detail is key to clear communication. Finish your illustration off by observing stitching lines, buttons, and rivets. Gold is the traditional choice but you can have fun by trying out other colors.

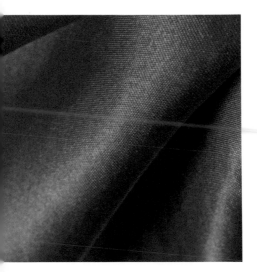

SATIN

Shiny fabrics reflect the light and show the influence of colors surrounding them. The light revealing the form creates a wide range of values; you may use four or five in the illustration. Colors that include the local color of the garment and the reflected color it picks up provide a way to enhance the illustration and add accents of color to the main garment. Determine where the light source is coming from and see the highlight and shadow shapes. Look for reflected light in the shadow area. Reflected satin has similar characteristics to leather, but satin will show thinner fold widths.

△ **Sharp edges**
The costumed figure wearing satin is illustrated by showing shiny, sharp edges between light and dark.

STEP 1
Start with a washy base of bleeding color. Concentrate the color in areas that would naturally contain shadows such as within folds and below features such as bows. Try applying a layer of clean water first and apply the paint or ink over the top while the paper is still wet.

STEP 2
Satin is a substantial and dense cloth—much more so than other shiny fabrics such as chiffon or organza. The addition of a darker tone into areas of the greatest shadow will make the fabric appear denser and more like satin.

STEP 3
Further enhance shadows once your work is completely dry by means of a dark pen or pencil line along the upper edges of the deepest folds and shadows.

We all have different personalities and look unique. So why would everyone want to illustrate things in the same manner? You want to find your style: it should be edgy, cool, and should make a point. List your likes and dislikes to begin exploring the process of style development. Avoid copying another style; this is a dead end and will lead to a return to basics. This chapter will open the door to creativity and style for you, and you should walk through this door on your own. The key is to trust you can do it and not waver in your search for individuality. Seek to inform your viewer and add a drop of humor into the recipe and you will be off and running.

CHAPTER

7

Creativity
and Style

Expressing *40* yourself

The opportunity to be creative with your projects exists with each piece you illustrate. The desire to find a personal style will push you to seek new ways to express your vision. Learning the rules about a subject will enhance the most important part of fashion illustration, which is finding your way.

FINDING YOUR STYLE

The way you choose to illustrate will be determined by current trends in illustration, what your collection looks like, the skill level you bring to the assignment, and what you find attractive. You might also be influenced by the work of another illustrator. This is a form of inspiration and should be encouraged—but not to the point of copying a style from someone else.

The main resource when it comes to finding a personal style is your life and experiences. You will do your best work when you are not worrying about it.

▷ **Learn the rules, break the rules**
Once you have mastered and understood the techniques required to communicate your ideas, you can then afford the luxury of breaking the rules and forging your own unique perspective.

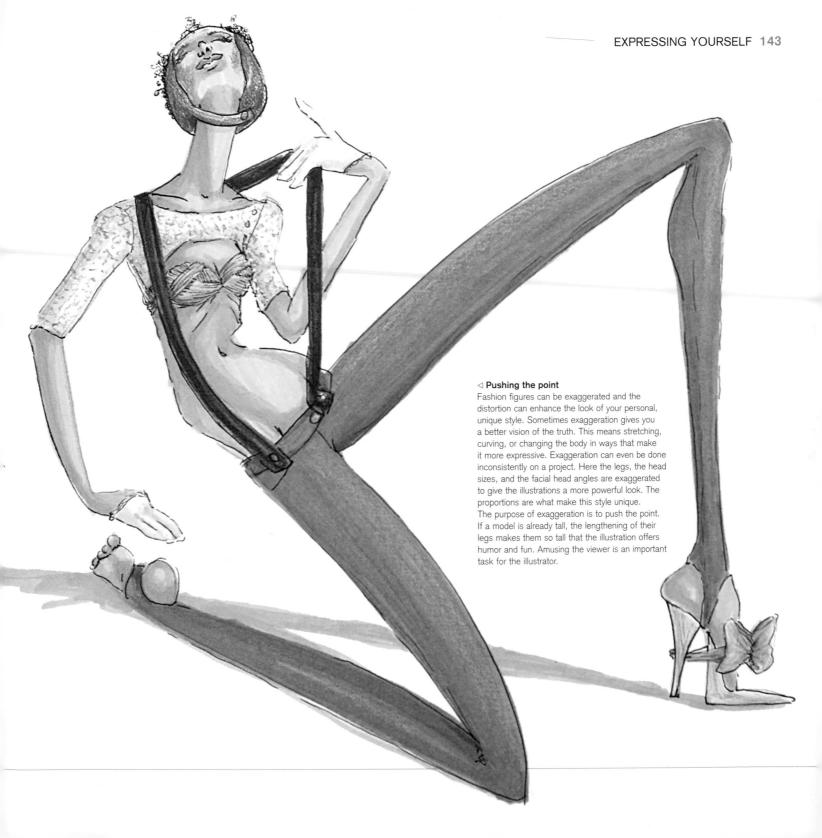

◁ **Pushing the point**

Fashion figures can be exaggerated and the distortion can enhance the look of your personal, unique style. Sometimes exaggeration gives you a better vision of the truth. This means stretching, curving, or changing the body in ways that make it more expressive. Exaggeration can even be done inconsistently on a project. Here the legs, the head sizes, and the facial head angles are exaggerated to give the illustrations a more powerful look. The proportions are what make this style unique. The purpose of exaggeration is to push the point. If a model is already tall, the lengthening of their legs makes them so tall that the illustration offers humor and fun. Amusing the viewer is an important task for the illustrator.

◁ ▽ **Folded paper scraps**
These illustrations are folded and constructed out of scraps of paper. The figures are drawn well, the colors are depicted with attractive harmony, and the simple materials are a unique way to illustrate differently. This is a perfect example of the way the use of materials can inspire a style.

THREE-DIMENSIONAL ILLUSTRATION AND UNIQUE MATERIALS

If you really start to think about it, many ideas will come along to help you illustrate in your style. Wad up a piece of paper and you could make a figure out of it. You might think sculpturally and illustrate in paper—a brilliant example of thinking creatively. The construction of a more raised surface and the use of unique materials is simple, yet clever.

THE MODEL

Most models convey an attitude. The empathy you feel for a model is part of the drawing process. If you work with a good model, you will find that illustrating and drawing will be easier. The importance of the model in fashion illustration cannot be underestimated: you are only as good as your model.

◁ **Choose a pose**
Remember to choose the pose that conveys what is important about your design. It may sometimes be preferable to select only part of the figure to represent your concept powerfully.

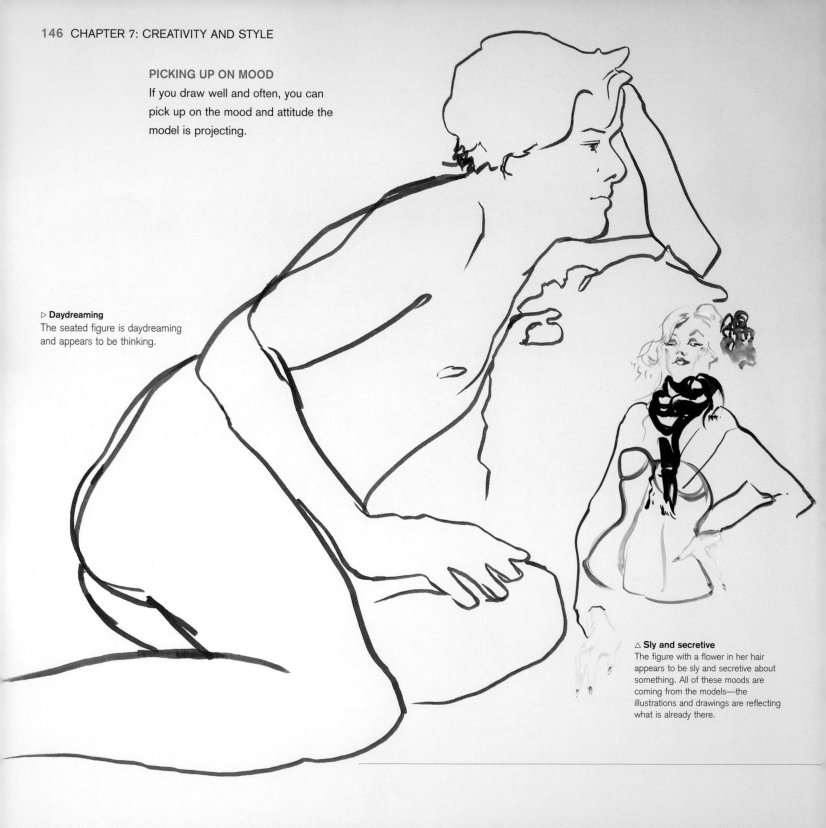

PICKING UP ON MOOD

If you draw well and often, you can pick up on the mood and attitude the model is projecting.

▷ **Daydreaming**
The seated figure is daydreaming and appears to be thinking.

△ **Sly and secretive**
The figure with a flower in her hair appears to be sly and secretive about something. All of these moods are coming from the models—the illustrations and drawings are reflecting what is already there.

◁ **Match model and clothes**
Everything about the figure should reinforce what you are trying to say about the clothes; the model should look like the kind of person who would feel comfortable in the outfit that you are illustrating.

◁ **Introduce movement**
This pose captures a moment in time like a snapshot. The figure has great movement and suggests a lively and fun attitude as she spins round so fast that she quite literally has to hold onto her hat.

◁ **Holding interest**
The red paper used as part of the shadow shapes on the flesh tones for the pastel figure is a unique color. A touch of surprise in the illustration will keep the viewer interested.

SELECTIVITY

Try zooming in on a view. Cropping an illustration is a time-honored tradition. Cut out one part or move to the left or right of the main page; adding or taking something out to arrive at the best possible spatial design. Work with an unusual color to convey a different color harmony. Or, leave out part of the drawing on the face and body so the viewer can "participate" in the drawing to complete the visual.

![ATTITUDE]()

ATTITUDE

◁ **Fiber-tip markers**
This figure is blowing a kiss to the crowd and in her exuberance she displays a humorous abandon. Humor is important in fashion illustration. To amuse and inform the viewer is the height of expression.

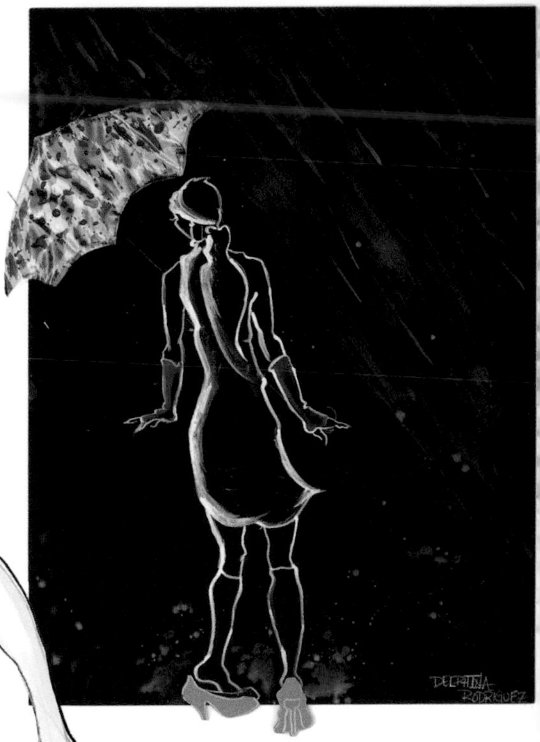

△ **White drawing**
The white brush and ink drawing was created on black paper—the mood is conveyed with blue textured paint applied with a dry brush.

◁ **Mixed media figure**
This figure with attitude was created with mixed media using fabric and drawn elements.

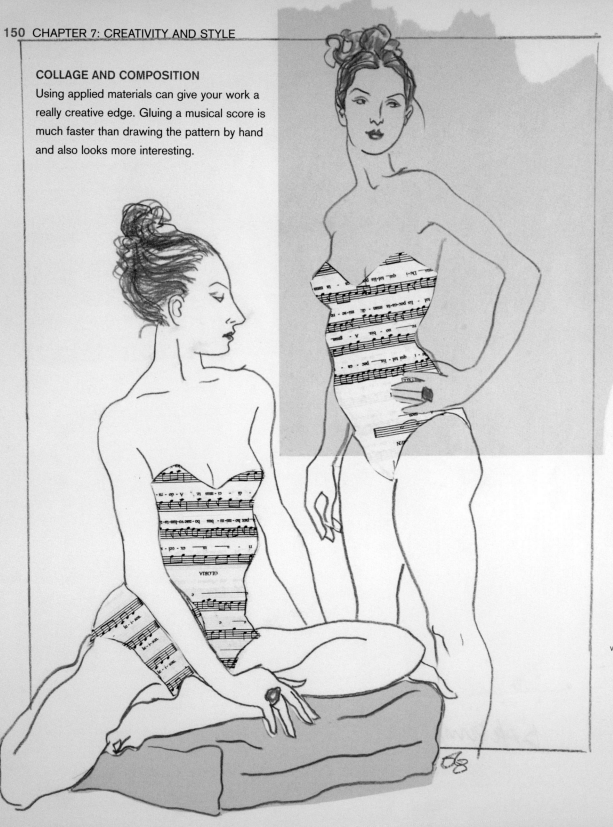

COLLAGE AND COMPOSITION

Using applied materials can give your work a really creative edge. Gluing a musical score is much faster than drawing the pattern by hand and also looks more interesting.

◁ **Working the background**
A tonally compatible collaged block in the background of the page will give your work an artistic feel and can create an interesting tension between the composition of the figures on the page.

Using a computer ▷
As well as physically gluing the layers of paper together, you can have fun scanning textures into the computer as well as your figures, and use software packages to combine everything together. This will result in a less bulky finished piece.

Working with a limited palette ▷
If there is a lot of textural interest within your work, try and be selective about the use of color to avoid information overload, and a drawing that appears too busy and cluttered.

▽ **Using color effectively**
The eye will always be attracted to an area of collage because it really stands out from the page, especially if the paper is in an attention-grabbing color. Use this to your advantage as a method of flagging up key elements within your design or to strengthen the silhouette by outlining the model.

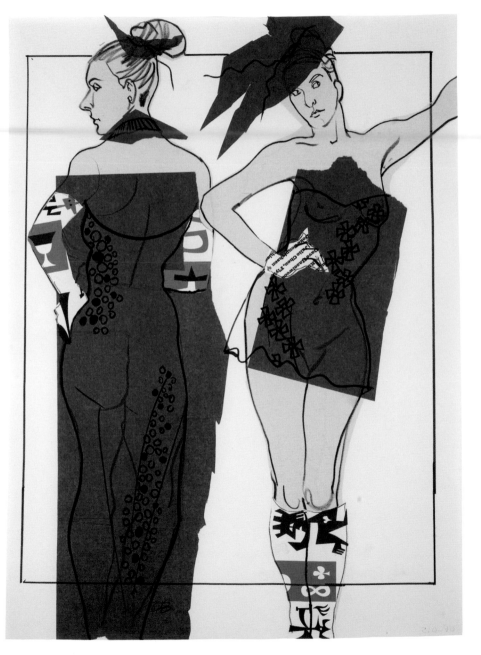

◁ **Make it dynamic**
Experiment with blocking areas of color from the range within the outfit that you are illustrating onto the page behind the figure for a lively energetic attitude.

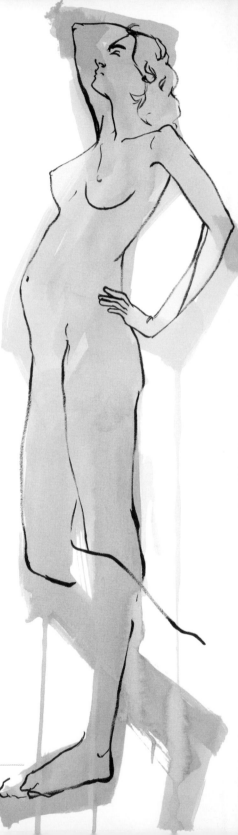

Break the rules ▷
Break the rules and break out of the outline with your coloring for a strong and bold statement.

COLOR ME UNCONVENTIONAL

From a carefully handpicked background that echoes the model's clothes to color work that spills over an outline's edge, use color as part of your artistic statement.

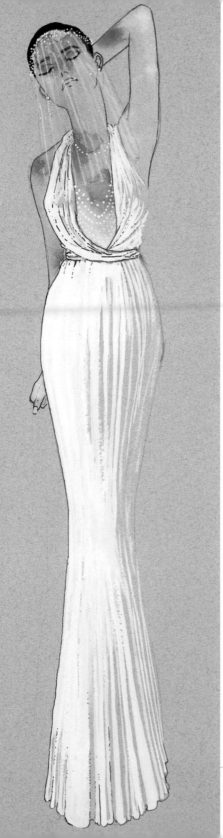

◁ **Dare to be unconventional**
The color applied to the figure in this illustration effectively reinvents what might otherwise be considered a fairly classic style of garment.

▽ **Unexpected touches**
The figure here is cropped and created with non-realistic colors. The blue hair is unexpected, and the texture in the background contrasts with the pale smoothness of the figure's flesh.

△ **Illustration and reality**
An illustration is the illusion of reality. Keep life drawings looking like a moment in time rather than a stuffy rendering that might as well be a photo.

▷**Yarn figure**
The yarn figure is full of interesting texture and the colors help add to the mood of love.

ABSTRACTION

Abstract shapes create visual style and interest. Abstraction can be based on layers and overlapping, use of cropping, unique materials, and line and shape contrasts.

△ **Abstract figure**
The more abstract figure is a pattern. Each of these artists came up with a different solution to illustrating. All of them draw well and the choice came down to materials and what would best convey the story quality of the illustration.

△ **Hidden message**
The overlapping figures in this illustration are combined with a text element tucked into the shapes. The text is a hidden message and adds something for the viewer to find.

△ **Mean and moody**
The sombre use of tonal inks really captures a mean and moody atmosphere in this illustration. Try experimenting with bleaching areas of ink out for an even more abstract effect.

Index

Bold page numbers refer to illustrations.

Credits

Quarto would like to thank the following artists for kindly supplying images for inclusion in this book:

Danielle Mussman, Jannika Lilja, Shawna Chan, Albert Ramos Cortes, Jacqi Ko, Jaedo Shim, Kaleo Magdaro, Nancy Delos Reyes, JR Watson, Catherine Janky, Dee Larsen, Murial Jordan, Martha Pelivanis, Amanda Kamm, Delphina Rodriguez, Dale Dombrowski, Margaret Yoha, and Mallory Kneller.